A CELEBRATION OF
LIFE AND LEGACY

PAULETTE V. DAVIDSON

www.xulonpress.com

DEDICATION

To the memories of my two moms:
Rosella Hurst Brown Poindexter
and
Elizabeth Cobbs Butler

CONTENTS

FOREWORD

R ev. Paulette Davidson has been our sister and friend for over forty-eight years. Evident in her character and from her heart, this woman of God has always found it necessary to make people aware of God's goodness, love, and grace relative to their lives. This author is no novice to pain and struggle. She learned at an early age that the only antidote for the difficulties of life itself is a profound and undeniable relationship with God through Jesus Christ our Lord.

The purpose of the stories in this book—each passage, each vignette, each expression—knowing what we do of the author, is to make free the hearts and minds of those bound by the trickery of demonic illusions. She strives to give hope to those who are in their season of suffering and to encourage all who do not know Jesus Christ. Clearly, it is her desire that all would come to the knowledge of Him and surrender their souls that they might have freedom from their past and an eternal life of victory.

This book reveals how God sustained this author even when she didn't know His perfect will for her life. Reverend Paulette has lived her entire life dependent on a God who has been responsive to her every need. He has allowed His servant the opportunity to see first-hand the awesomeness of His authority in the earth realm. Yes, even today you would say "wow!" at her struggling childhood, and we would agree. Yet amidst what would seem daunting, this writer found herself looking unto Jesus and being rescued by Him to the safety of His bosom.

The scars were many; however, the ability to find growth, purpose, and more than anything else the power to *forgive* demonstrates her awareness of God's grace. Forgiveness is the key in all humanity's ability to move beyond the areas of pain we have endured. Being able to forgive both ourselves and those who have created suffering in our lives brings healing.

We can't even begin to understand the impact of the child welfare system that existed during the author's childhood. Yet we can assure you that once Paulette came to Miracle Temple Church, she became one of the young people of our ministry and from that time on was part of our extended family. The youth network at that ministry was second to none and relevant in our lives, even until this day. A large cluster of us have remained friends and family, which has proven to be instrumental in our individual growth, successes, and life's influences. We all still love one another and our God.

When we pontificate on our sister and friend's demeanor and person, we understand with clarity that she is attempting to impress upon each reader that in relationships, and especially those with foster children, the following considerations should be taken into account:

*   Couples must first make sound decisions in choosing a mate.
*   Teach, nurture, and love your children, no matter what.
*   Tough it out when adversity presents stress in relationships.
*   Men must be in a position to parent any children that they bring into this world.

*   Pray that the life choices you make are excellent so that you won't become guilty of the potential destruction of a child's mental, emotional, or physical well-being as a result of your inability to stay together after fantasizing about being in an adult relationship.

Greater in the scheme of this book is the very foundation that began the work to make the author whole, and that is a serious relationship with God. He is King of Kings and Lord of Lords in her life. Without this transition in her life, she would be clueless as to what she should be doing or where her life would be today. The Bible states in Psalm 103:5, "Who satisfieth thy mouth with good things; so that thy youth is renewed like the eagle's" (KJV). Reverend Paulette has found redemption in her relationship with her God. He, Father God, has restored her paths that she might become the restorer of the breach, as referenced in Isaiah 58:12. Now she is a godly representative who is crying out in the wilderness, proclaiming liberty for the masses.

Be blessed by the efforts of this anointed writer who has shared words regarding her early life experiences that they might hit a nerve to comfort, make many think, and make all aware that life is to be celebrated no matter what the toil. That's the way God planned it!

With abundant love forever,
Reverends Drs. Barry and Melinda Story,
Senior pastors and founders
Restored Paths Ministries, Inc.

THE HOSPITAL

I t was Friday night. This long workweek would soon be over for the third shift nursing staff, as it was almost midnight. Although their shift was still young, their weekend would begin at the end of this shift. The routine chaos of the day was finally settling, and the wards were beginning to quiet down. This spring night on the west side of Philadelphia was no different from any other evening, or so the nurses and other employees thought. However, at Philadelphia General Hospital, May 30, 1952, would become a night that not many of them would ever forget.

The hospital staff anticipated another calm evening of caring for the needs of their patients and interacting with each other. Several more ticks on the wall clock positioned near the nurses' station and May 30 would seal itself shut.

Rosella tried to remain calm and still as cautioned, but it was becoming increasingly difficult. Day after day of waiting was becoming too much for her to bear. It had been thirty days now. Rosella didn't know how she would sanely be able to go into another month of waiting to give birth. When her water broke on May 1, and her being only eight months the doctors were watching her condition closely. Rosella's thoughts were centered on a speedy

13

delivery, a healthy baby and, *Oh, Lord, help me make it through with this new baby.*

Having been restricted to bed rest for thirty days in a maternity ward, it was easy for her to lose count of the number of births going on around her. Rosella's thoughts quickly shifted from pleasant thoughts to great alarm. When would her baby come? Rosella had contracted an infection during the delay of delivery of this pregnancy. Her doctors had warned her that the infection in her body, too long-named to remember, had affected her baby. Initially, they believed there was a good chance that the baby would survive the infection, but they were now of the opinion that the baby had not survived the infection.

To the doctors, Rosella's health had become paramount in this medical case, as they felt the baby was already lost. "Rosella," the doctors stated, "it seems that your baby is already deceased. We will return shortly to remove the dead baby so that you can live."

As the doctors just coldly began to walk away, Rosella began screaming, pleading, crying, and praying. "No! No! No! This cannot happen!" Rosella began protectively holding her stomach, and the nurses tried to calm her down as best they could. They were trying to persuade her to accept the doctors' directions and to calm herself for her own good. Day after day, they had seen the hope in Rosella's eyes of birthing her baby. *Maybe today will be the day. Maybe my baby will come today.* Shift after shift, they had witnessed the despair in her spirit. Some of the nurses were thinking about requesting a transfer to a different ward, as it was becoming increasingly difficult to face Rosella day after day without any change in medical progress.

Rosella tried to comply with remaining calm and still after the nurses had left her. Alone and crying, Rosella began to talk to

God. "God, this can't be happening. I want my baby!" she cried. She remembered the doctors' instructions. "They think my baby is dead, and they are going to return after dinner and remove my baby. No, God, no," Rosella pleaded. Rosella thought about the story in the Bible where God formed man from the dust of the ground and breathed into his nostrils the breath of life, and man became a living soul. She did not know, nor did she care, that the story was found in Genesis 2:7. All Rosella knew was that God had breathed into man and man became a living soul.

The doctors had presented Rosella with the health concerns for her life, and she knew the effect that the situation could have on her unborn child. Intellectually, Rosella understood well. Emotionally and with the heart of a mother, it was an entirely different story. It seemed that all was lost. In an attempt to calm herself, Rosella began to mentally chronicle the last few weeks.

April 30, 1952 ticktocked into May 1 without challenge. I experienced some discomfort throughout the night, but that was to be expected at eight months of pregnancy. By midafternoon on that Thursday, my water broke, and my friends rushed me to the hospital. My other two children were safe with friends, and James, the baby's father, was with me.

Multiple hours later, my labor had calmed, and the baby didn't seem to be in a hurry to exit my womb. A few hours later, my baby's father needed to leave. He left with promises from the doctor that he would be contacted at the first signs of delivery.

My baby's daddy called the nursing station the next day and many days following, all to the same statement: "Mr. Geiger, there has been no change. No baby yet. Rosella is doing as well as can be expected. We will let her know you called."

After the second and third week of no change, we were all very alarmed by my situation. Occasionally my friends would bring my children for a visit, and James would visit. Most importantly, we could not figure out why there was this incredible delay. The doctors offered little consolation. Finally, the doctors talked with us and decided to just wait a few more days. Those few more days had turned into weeks, and here we were at day thirty. The doctors had reached their limit, and now they were off having dinner, plotting how to remove my child from me in hopes of saving my life. Oh my God, please help me.

Call it a vision, a hope, a dream, or a mother experiencing deleterious pain, but Rosella knew that this child would be born. She couldn't explain it—she didn't know how—but she just knew that her child would be born, not taken. Yes, maybe her baby would have a few health issues as a result of the infection, but her child would be born. She just knew it. She felt that she had an assurance from God. *He breathed life into the first man; surely He can breathe life into my baby,* she thought.

Just as Rosella was drifting into a calm sleep, mild contractions began to come upon her. Suddenly she began to feel something from inside, and this commotion began to increase and become more intense. Rosella had birthed other children, so she knew something was coming. She protectively cradled her abdomen and yelled for the nurse. Through panting breaths, Rosella tried to tell the nurse what she felt. The nurse tried to tell Rosella that everything was still the same. "You don't feel anything. You're just experiencing shock from the information. You don't feel anything." The nurse thought Rosella was delirious and tried to convince her to calm and settle herself.

Rosella continued to cry out: "Something is happening; please help me." The nurse lifted the sheets to once again check to assure Rosella that nothing had changed, and she began to scream, jumping up and down. "Oh, my Lord," the nurse squealed, "a baby is coming. Oh, my Lord, call the doctor—a baby is coming."

The doctors bolted from their scheduled dinner break to the bedside of the patient who had been dubbed "Day Thirty, No Change." As the doctors hurried along, their thoughts were, *What on earth is happening? What is this woman experiencing now? We know the baby is already dead. It's no wonder that the infection from the mother infected the fetus. What is all this commotion about? Dinner is getting cold over another false alarm.*

All of a sudden, change had come. The doctors performed a quick check to assure everyone that this was just another false alarm and that they would return shortly to complete the medical procedure. However, to their surprise, Rosella was indeed in labor. A baby was about to be born against all the odds of the medical team and medical science. *How could this happen?* the doctors thought. *This is too risky!* They tried to reassure themselves, but God had a plan in motion.

Finally, on day thirty, without grandmother, baby's father, or other children around to witness it, this baby who had lain dormant for thirty days fought her way into this world. Dr. James Alesbury proclaimed, "It's a girl, live at 11:58 p.m.!" Through a sweat-soaked face, grinning with pride, pleasure, and confidence, the girl's mother, Rosella, exclaimed, "And her name is Paulette Virginia Brown Poindexter!"

Paulette was very, very tiny at birth and indeed suffered from the infection carried by Rosella, her mother. At Paulette's birth, the doctors noted that she had blindness in both eyes and would experience epilepsy throughout her life. Paulette was so tiny that her mother said she could fit into a pint-sized Hellmann's mayonnaise jar with the lid on top. The doctors were uncertain whether the blindness would be permanent or temporary.

Several days after giving birth, Rosella had healed well from that incredible thirty-day ordeal and was released to go home. However, tiny baby Paulette would remain hospitalized for many more days to come.

Baby Paulette's world became the warm plastic bin of an incubator, with soft lights revealing her every movement. Each day Paulette became stronger and put on more weight; her cries grew louder and louder. No longer were the nurses alerted of Paulette's needs by the weak and feeble wailings of an infant struggling to hold on to life. Paulette's cries had become full-throated, determined cries of requests to be fed, changed, and held.

Rosella faithfully visited her pint-sized Paulette, and sometimes she would bring her other children along for the visit. Finally, after months of inpatient treatment, Paulette reached her maximum of hospital care. Paulette's demands via crying were becoming more than the nursing staff could handle. Her needs shifted from medical needs to nurturing needs.

The nurses cherished Paulette and were sad to have her depart, but they really needed to attend to their other infant patients. Paulette kept the nurses busier than any two babies on the ward. Besides, Paulette had reached the stage where what she needed was love, care, and nurturing from her own family. Paulette's medical journey had reached its limit in the baby ward of PGH, also known as Philadelphia General Hospital.

Having been born blind and experiencing epilepsy, Paulette would have many, many doctor appointments to follow her development and progress. Rosella asked the eye doctor, "Is it possible to give my baby Paulette my eyes?"

The physician understood Rosella's heart as a mother but assured her, "No, that is not possible. Besides, your daughter needs you to be able to see to help her through this life."

Rosella had many struggles throughout her life both before and after Paulette was born and came home. In fact, it was felt that the infection Rosella had during the thirty-day hospital stay may have been the result of alcohol poisoning.

I am Paulette. This is the story of the lives of my mother, Rosella; my grandmother, Pauline; and me. Watch as the hand of God intricately weaves the fabric of our lives and many of the lives we come in contact with. Journey with me as I unfold the legacy of Pauline Virginia Hurst Brown, the matriarch of the Hurst-Brown-Poindexter family.

HER MOTHER'S DEATH MOVED HER ON

————◦-⊛♥⊛-◦————

My mom, Rosella Hurst Brown, was the only child of my grandmother. I never met my grandmother, Pauline Virginia Hurst Brown. She had gone on to glory years before I was born. But my mother decided that I would be worthy to carry her mother's name, even though I am named Paulette. It was the month of May, and Mother's Day was special to my mother. Since I was born in May, Mom wanted me named after her mother. However, Mom preferred the name *Paulette* over the name *Pauline*, so I was named Paulette Virginia Brown Poindexter.

Grandma Pauline's life was short-lived. The stories I was told were that Grandma Pauline had suffered with hypertension, which led to cardiac failure. Grandma Pauline, born on January 25, 1908, died at the very young age of thirty-six on October 3, 1944. At the time, she had been living in Harrisburg, Pennsylvania, with her husband.

My mom's father was never a part of her life. Grandma Pauline married Mr. William Brown of Harrisburg, and Mr. Brown accepted my mom, Rosella, as his own child. My mom was around eighteen months old when her mom and Mr. Brown got married.

As an adult, I asked Mr. Brown if he had ever legally adopted my mom and if he had any documents to that effect to support her last name as Brown. He said back in those days, since he and Pauline were married, no one ever asked for any papers or documents regarding Rosella's name. He said he had been able to enroll her in school as Rosella Brown, because of their marriage.

When my grandmother, Pauline, died, the story is told, that my mother, Rosella, became anxious and wanted to move away from Harrisburg. She felt alone and overwhelmed with responsibilities. She had a one-year-old daughter named Madelyn Carol. Rosella had no siblings and no mother, and the only father she had ever known was Mr. Brown. He was a kind man, but she needed more; she was searching for more. Rosella thought, *If I could just relocate to Philadelphia, I could start over, start fresh, start new. Maybe my stepdad would allow me to leave Madelyn Carol with him, and I'll come back to get her when I get settled in Philadelphia.*

Just when my mom had worked up enough courage to ask such a mammoth request of her stepdad, she was stopped before she could get started. Mr. Brown knew his stepdaughter, Rosella, quite well. They had been in each other's lives for over eighteen years. Mr. Brown was a kind and quiet man. He spoke very little, but when he did, his words generally resonated with instruction. After a long day of errands and just being busy outside the house, Rosella came in late one evening. When she entered the home, Mr. Brown invited her to sit down with him in the front room of the home to chat for a while.

Mr. Brown started: "Rosella, I know you miss your mother. I miss her too, and I know things will never be the same for you without her around. I know that you are frightened and uncertain about how things will unfold for you and your baby. I know that you have been

21

giving thought to what you should do next. I can see that you want to leave and that you are trying to figure that out. Let me help you.

"I know you want to leave Madelyn Carol here while you go off someplace new to start over, but that will not work. I know you expect to be gone for a few weeks and then come back to get her, but you're only nineteen years old and not much more than a baby yourself.

"You can go. You can leave and start over wherever you see fit, but you cannot leave Madelyn Carol here with me. You know the number of times you would leave her here with promises to be back in a couple of hours, which stretched into a couple of days and then into weekends. You cannot continue to do that to the child.

"Consider this: You go, but you leave Madelyn Carol behind. Yes, leave her behind. Allow her to be adopted by loving, caring people who already know and love her. You know that Buddy and Anna would be willing to adopt Madelyn Carol and raise her as their own child. She loves them, and you know that they love her from the many times she has already stayed at their house."

Rosella sat silently, trying to sort through all this information. Mr. Brown was giving her the opportunity to be free, virtually childless, while her baby daughter would be loved and cared for by his relatives. Mr. Buddy, whose real name was Cornelius, was Mr. Brown's brother. Uncle Buddy and Aunt Anna were good people. They had always been good to her and to her baby, Madelyn Carol. In many ways this was an answer to a nineteen-year-old's life, but in other ways, it would mean permanent separation from her only daughter. It didn't matter that Uncle Buddy and Aunt Anna were relatives and that Madelyn Carol would remain in the family. It still meant that Madelyn Carol would be raised to call someone else "Mom."

Mr. Brown spoke comfortingly and said, "Rosella, you have to be an adult now. Why don't you think about all of this for a few days before you make your move? We just want what's best for you and for your baby."

Rosella didn't get much sleep that night. *Oh, how I miss Mom,* she sighed to herself. She lay awake, staring into the depths of the darkness, trying to decide what she should do. Madelyn Carol was only one year old. *Will she remember me?* she wondered. *When I visit her, will she consider me a stranger? Will she remember our bond? Will she ever forgive me for giving her up?* Rosella's thoughts tossed her through the night. As night ticktocked into daybreak, Rosella knew intellectually what she must do. She now had to convince her heart to go along with her decision.

Rosella knew that Uncle Buddy and his wife, Aunt Anna, could not have children of their own. She knew that the Browns had always been good and kind to Madelyn Carol, and she knew that her daughter would be well cared for; but none of that consoled her breaking heart. Would her daughter know her, recognize her, remember her, love her in three, five, seven, ten years?

With a heavy and sad heart, Rosella agreed to the adoption, all the while wondering if she had made the right decision. Those were very sad and quiet days in my mom's life. Immediately after signing the papers releasing her firstborn, Madelyn Carol Brown, to her uncle and aunt, Mr. and Mrs. Cornelius and Anna Brown, my mom, Rosella Hurst Brown, boarded a Greyhound bus to Philadelphia. That was probably the longest, hardest, and saddest two-hour bus ride of my mother's life.

When the Greyhound bus driver announced their arrival in Philadelphia, also known as the City of Brotherly Love, my mom felt a glimmer of hope. Mom's hope was that maybe she could make this all work out for good somehow.

In the great city of Philadelphia, there was a family who had just recently experienced a tragedy regarding their youngest daughter. As a result, this family had posted a notice of Room for Rent on a sign in the window of their home. Shortly after Rosella got off the bus and glanced through a few of the city maps that she had found in the racks at the station, she hailed a hack to take her to where she would be going next.

Actually, Rosella didn't have any idea of where to go next. She decided that she had been kept safe this far; she would take a chance and ask for help. The hack driver who answered her hail was a gentleman who introduced himself as Mr. Mitchell. As it happened, Mr. Mitchell knew of a family that was looking for someone to rent a room. When Rosella asked the driver if he knew of any place safe she could get a room, he smiled and said, "Young lady, today is a great day. I know just the place for you."

Rosella and Mr. Mitchell piled her few belongings into his station wagon, and she settled back as she was driven to the Cobbs family residence. Mr. Mitchell informed Rosella of the name of the family offering the room for rent. He said, "They are the Cobbs family, and they are good people."

Months prior to Rosella's arrival in Philadelphia, Mrs. Jennie Cobbs had slumped over in the living room chair, still holding the telephone in disbelief. The voice on the other end of the phone said that they were calling from the home for girls. This institution had entered the Cobbses' lives because their youngest daughter, Frances, had a violent dislike for going to school.

Frances Cobbs, aged fifteen, had reached her maximum number of truancies, and the Philadelphia School Board had declared her a truant and placed her in an institution that would make her go to school. As always, Frances had an aversion to authority, and just like she wouldn't listen to her mother, she did not want to listen to the authorities at the girls' home.

The voice of the caller, Mr. Wayne or Mr. Crane or whatever he said his name was, was numbed out by the startling realization that her baby girl was now gone forever. The male voice continued: "I regret to inform you that we believe Frances committed suicide because she was unhappy with following the rules at the home."

Even in her grief-stricken fog, Mrs. Cobbs felt that something about that story did not ring entirely true. Rumors of murder surfaced, and following an investigation and police reports, the lawyers involved wanted to drag the case on and on, either attempting to cash in on a family's grief or to protect an institution. Neither motive was very clear to Mrs. Cobbs.

When her lawyer recommended that she place the family residence up as collateral to continue her legal battle with the girls' home, Mrs. Cobbs felt it was time to let it go. She could not place her family in jeopardy of losing their home, along with all the other grief they had experienced. Although Mrs. Cobbs was willing to walk away from this legal battle for the security and safety of her remaining family, she knew in her heart that her daughter Frances could not and would not have ever committed suicide.

Through the weeks, Mrs. Cobbs was able to slowly reenter the world around her, along with her other children. Mrs. Cobbs felt the need for a fresh, new start. The Cobbs family's new start began with a simple sign, which read, "Room for Rent."

My mom, Rosella Hurst Brown, fresh off the bus from Harrisburg, having just lost her only daughter to adoption, rang Mrs. Cobbs's doorbell, seeking to occupy the room that was for rent. Mr. Mitchell accompanied Mom to the door as he assisted her with her belongings. Mr. Mitchell smiled and greeted Elizabeth when she opened the door. As it turned out, the Cobbs family knew Mr. Mitchell well, and everyone called him "Uncle Mitchell." Elizabeth grinned and said, "Hi, Uncle Mitchell."

When Elizabeth Cobbs, aged twenty, answered the door, after being excited about seeing Uncle Mitchell, she spoke kindly to Rosella. Uncle Mitchell volunteered that Rosella was there about the room for rent. Guardedly Mom spoke up and said, "My name is Rosella Hurst Brown Poindexter," and then she repeated, "I came to inquire about the room you have for rent, and I am wondering if the room is still available." Elizabeth turned and called to her mother, saying, "Mom, Uncle Mitchell is here, and this young lady wants to rent the room."

That's where it started. Right then, that day, Elizabeth and Rosella became fast friends. After my mom rented the room and the girls discovered that they were just a year apart in age and celebrated birthdays in the same month of February, they became inseparable. They were sisters. Rosella, an only child, now had a sister, and Elizabeth, who had recently buried a younger sister, opened her life to a new sister.

Mom and Elizabeth remained close, dedicated sisters throughout the remainder of their lives. As young children, we called Elizabeth "Aunt Liz," of course, because she was Mom's sister. We never knew that Mom and Aunt Liz were not blood sisters until I was a teenager. Later in our lives, we referred to Mom's sister-friend Elizabeth as "Granny." Other friends referred to her as "Momma Liz."

When Elizabeth Cobbs answered the ring of the doorbell and encountered Rosella on that first day, neither of them knew at that time that the relationship that was about to be formed was God's plan for their lives. Their friendship, their sisterhood, would somehow play out in the lives of their children for years to come.

My mom found employment through the Pennsylvania Railroad. Mom was part of a team that cleaned out the cars, and she began to feel established in Philadelphia. Although Rosella and Elizabeth had "sistered" each other, and Mrs. Cobbs had become a surrogate mother for Rosella, her thoughts daily wondered about her daughter, Madelyn Carol. Rosella wondered, *Is Madelyn Carol happy and healthy? Will she remember me? Will she remember that I am her mom? Will she ever forgive me for giving her away?*

Alcohol was a frequent seasoning throughout Rosella's life. It was probably a coping crutch she relied on to quiet her emotional pain through the loss of her mother and baby. Now having two older children, a new baby with special needs, and limited help available from family and friends, life was difficult for Rosella. Some years later, it became necessary for Rosella's children to be placed in the foster care system when she was arrested for larceny.

With Rosella in jail, DeWitt, aged five; Joyce, aged four; and I had to endure the foster care system. I was one and a half years old when we entered into foster care. An eighteen-month-old blind child with epilepsy presented with extraordinary needs in the foster care system. Yes, a child with special needs brought in a higher dollar figure, but it also brought greater needs, responsibilities, and complexities.

I had frequent medical appointments because of my diagnosis, and one great follow-up appointment revealed a significant truth: the blindness was temporary and could be treated! I would indeed have vision. My vision was restored, but the demon of epilepsy raged on.

Foster placement is an animal in and of itself. Such placements often present as a cruel evil cloaked in the necessity of care for those who qualify and who often become victims by that very system. A multitude of quotes surround the child-care system. It has been said, "Hurt people, hurt people," "Once a victim, always a victim," and "Once in *that* system, your life is messed up forever." Historically, there is probably a great deal of truth in those statements; however, let's not jump to conclusions just yet.

Let's take a journey. First, foster care placement was an ultimate nightmare for me. Second, epilepsy demonized my body for a number of years, paralleling the biblical account of the episodes. Third, salvation and redemption can be found in the foster care system. Being separated from your mother and siblings at an early age is extremely traumatic. Now add in the ingredients of unfamiliar surroundings, unfriendly faces, and unfamiliar voices; or even worse, smiling faces that tear your heart, life, and body to shreds.

My heart was flung into the homes of over twenty different sets of foster caregivers. I probably frequented so many homes as a result of my medical needs. No one could deal with my seizures. They were diagnosed as grand-mal seizures. I was on much medication, but I still experienced seizures quite often.

We were instructed to call the female parent of these homes "Mom," even though we had a mom. This did not always go over well with the birth children living in the home. These kids didn't want strangers calling their mother "Mom." Because I knew I already had a mom, I would say the word *mom* to these ladies, but only as the lady of the house, rather than as my mom.

You never knew what to expect behind each new foster door. But as much as you didn't know what to expect, you also did know that there were some things you could count on. The foster care system, proud of its history, provided the usual family things like a place to sleep, clothes, regular feedings, diaper changes, baths, toys, etc., and sometimes you felt you were being well provided for. Sure, every kid's inherent hope is to be full, clean, dry, protected, and, in a perfect world, happy. Sometimes you got all those things; other times you got only one or two of those hopes fulfilled. One thing you quickly learned from an early age in the foster system, even though you didn't understand it, was that nothing lasts forever.

Things were always changing. You were switched from one foster placement to another without a moment's notice. You could go to school from one foster home in the morning and end up in a different foster home after school. When the final school bell would ring, I would often wonder, *Where will I end up this afternoon?* Foster siblings changed all the time, and the rules were the worst. The rules changed at every house. The foster parents did not care that you were a lonely, frightened child whose life had been wedged apart by decisions made by selfish adults. All the foster parents knew was that you were under their care, which to them meant you were under their power; they were getting paid for you, and you were their property.

"Grow-up" was quick in these placements. You had to be careful to never bring the rules from the last place into the new place. That could get you punished. It was also important not to ask too many questions. That could also get you punished. Birth children in these foster homes utilized every opportunity to demonstrate the "king of the hill" syndrome and make you complete their chores or homework or blame you for their despicable behavior.

FOSTER CARE BETWEEN THE AGES OF ONE AND A HALF AND THIRTEEN YEARS OLD

—————— ·•· ❦❦❦ ·•· ——————

WATER CALL

In one house that I lived in, the lady of the house would go to church a couple of times during the week. Sometimes she went to Bible study, and other times she went to choir rehearsal. We did not go with her all the time during the week, but we went on Sundays. I say *we* because there were other children living in this home as well. Before the mom would leave home, we all had to have all of our chores completed, homework done, clothes ready for school, and be in bed. She would make sure that we were in bed before she left.

She would leave us in the house with an adult. He was her husband, a deacon in their church. This deacon was always dressed up as if he had someplace special to go, but he seldom left home unless it was to go to church. Deacon walked with a limp and seldom went upstairs. Once the mom had left for church, the deacon frequently called me and another foster girl downstairs. He would ask us to get him things, like water or something to eat from the fridge.

After we would get what he told us, he would then say to us, "Sit on Daddy's lap." He said it was to keep him company while he ate or drank whatever we had brought him. We would sit on his lap, and he would start with small talk about how our day had been and how school was progressing.

After he got us comfortable talking about school, he would rub the tops of our pajamas and then slide his hand down under our panties. The first time this happened, I jumped off his lap and started to scream. He slapped his big heavy hand over my mouth and gritted in my ear, "If you scream again, I am going to tell my wife that you got up after she left to get some more food, and you know what she will do to you." He grabbed me and forcefully pulled me back to him. His voice got really mean, and he said, "Sit here and shut up."

I sat there with tears streaming down my face and wondering, *What is he doing, and why is he doing this to me? It hurts. Why won't he stop?"* After he finished with us, he smiled and said, "Go on back to bed now." The other young girl was also crying, but she was afraid to resist Deacon. He told us not to say anything to Mother, because we were just playing games. I could never figure out what kind of game it was that we were playing. I did not enjoy this game. In fact, I hated it.

Weekly Deacon would call us. Each night, whenever the mom went to church, in fear I would wonder, *When is Deacon going to do his water call?* One night the deacon called us down to him, each by name, but we decided not to answer him. He continued to call us, but we continued to not answer him. Finally, he stopped calling us that night, and we never again went downstairs at night to him.

A few weeks after we refused to go downstairs to answer Deacon's water call, he got sick. I could hear the mother on the phone talking to people about his being sick. A few days later, he died. Mother explained to us that Deacon would not be coming back; he had died and was with Jesus. All of us foster kids got new clothes to wear to the funeral.

As I attended the funeral and the grave site, I watched as they lowered Deacon into the grave opening. His wife was crying and crying. She seemed so sad. I wondered, *Did she know what Deacon did to us? Should I tell her now since Deacon is gone?* She was sobbing and was so heartbroken. Then I realized that whatever Deacon had done to us, I didn't even know what to call it. I didn't know how to explain it. The mother was crying so hard that she probably would have told me it was my fault.

A couple of days after the funeral, we were all moved to other homes. I never saw the other foster girl again. We seldom knew the reasons behind the moves in foster placement. We just knew that pillowcases, garbage bags, and old suitcases were always at our fingertips. My thoughts were off and running: *Here we go again. Where to now? Who and what will be waiting for me there? What is going to happen next?*

BEAUTIFUL HOUSE

Many of the over twenty homes that I was placed in were ordinary homes intended to care for your needs while there. Most of these homes were modest, clean, and comfortable. All the homes required that we have a bed to ourselves. Sometimes I had more than one roommate, and other times I had a room to myself because of my epilepsy.

But there was one spectacular house I was placed in. It was beautiful inside and out. One would say that it looked like a page from a magazine. Everything always looked new and in its place. It was a very big house with a lot of rooms. There were three or four other foster children at this home during the time that I was placed there.

That home is where I learned not to be impressed by appearances. All those beautiful rooms were merely a showcase. All those rooms were off limits to us kids. There were two exceptions to our not being permitted in those beautiful rooms. Absolutely, we were permitted entrance when it was time to clean those rooms or whenever the case workers would visit. We, of course, had to keep those showcase rooms spotless because the agency visitations took place in the great front room.

If we were caught in those rooms for any other reason, we would be beaten or yelled at. Even the functional rooms like the kitchen and dining room were off limits to us. There was, however, a special place where we kids could eat and enjoy our meals—the basement steps. Yes, in that big beautiful house, we were restricted to eating our meals on the basement steps in very dim lighting. We had to go sit on the steps, and our plates would be handed to us. We weren't even permitted to walk across the kitchen to the steps, holding our plates. All our meals were eaten in that location. Just like dogs, we knew where to expect our meals. We would go straight to the "hole" to wait for our rations.

We were cautioned prior to a visit from the case workers about how to respond to their questions. Of course, we were threatened that if we didn't say and respond to the case workers like we were instructed, we would be taken out of the home and sent back to where we had come from.

We always had to be dressed nicely, and our hair had to look decent. The mom would always insist that we wash our faces and brush our teeth just before the case workers came to the house. The doorbell would ring, and the mom of the home would answer the door and allow the people to come in.

The case workers always introduced themselves. For the record, they would say, "We are from the Women's Christian Alliance, and we have come to check on the children." The case workers usually came in twos. They would say to us children individually things like, "Tell me, Paulette, do you like living here? Are Mom and Dad nice to you? Are you happy? Are you getting enough food to eat? Is there anything that you would like to tell us?"

We knew our answers could only be the sentences we had rehearsed for each question. I would perk up, smile, and answer, "Yes, madam, I like it here. Yes, madam, Mom and Dad are nice to me. Yes, madam, I am happy here. Yes, madam, I get enough food to eat every day," and finally, "No, madam" to the last question. All the other kids would respond in the same way. Even as bad as it may have been at a house, we seldom wanted to move because we at least knew what we had where we were. We never knew what we would encounter at a new place.

I used to sit there, hoping against hope that the case workers would see something, anything, on my face as a dead giveaway that I was actually unhappy there. But I guess they only saw the smile, or maybe seeing the smile made their day easier. Nonetheless, I remained hopeful that at least one of them would see past my plastered smile. They didn't. At least, they never acted like they did or never did anything or asked any deeper questions. They would just smile, make notes on their clipboards, put their papers and pens

away, stand up, shake hands with the mom of the house, and continue smiling as they walked out the door, promising to visit again.

Usually the case workers came just before lunch, so as soon as
they left, we trotted over to the basement steps and sat expectantly
waiting for our plates so we could eat lunch. As usual, we received
only one serving of food, and it was often small. We were always
hungry, but never allowed to ask for seconds.

While we were on the steps eating, I would often wish that the
case workers had forgotten something and would ring the doorbell
again and need to come back into the house to get it. Then they would
see that all of us kids had disappeared. Maybe the case workers
would wonder where we had all gone, since they would be able to
see and smell food on the stove. Would they wonder where we had
gone, not seeing us seated in the dining room or kitchen, knowing
that it was lunchtime? Would they say to the mom of the house, "We
have just one more question for the children"? Would they look for
us all through the house? Would they come and check the steps and
see us seated there in semidarkness, eating small amounts of food,
like dogs?

Oh, well. It never happened like that. That was just more of my
busy imagination at work, more of what was necessary to help me
pass the days while in that horrible system. We knew that the foster
parents were receiving money for taking care of us, but where did
all that money go? Wherever the money went, we children were the
labor that kept that particular house beautiful.

The Women's Christian Alliance agency probably meant well
and was probably a good organization to many people. But some
of us and our problems went unnoticed. The same sob story continues today: too many children with needs and not enough families

or money. Unfortunately, something has to be overlooked or left undone. Someone has to do without. As a child, I was just tired of it always being me.

The agency often provided new clothes for us children. They probably thought they were cleverly saving money, but what they were actually doing was identifying every kid in the system through one single act. Casual bystanders could spot and identify you as being a kid in the system simply by your clothes. You might as well have had a bull's-eye painted on your chest, because all the clothes provided by the agency were cut from the same bolts of material. Several outfits for boys and girls would be of the same fabric and design, but with different patterns. As a result, you were a target for ridicule and abuse.

JESUS, BE A FENCE ALL AROUND ME

My dad's name was William James Geiger. That's who I knew him as. I found out later that sometimes he also went by the name James William Geiger. My mom always called him James. My dad owned a candy store on South Street in South Philadelphia, and we loved it when he brought us candy. Whenever Dad would bring candy to the foster homes, he always brought enough for all the kids.

It was always a treat when I could ride in Dad's car. My favorite riding position was to kneel on the backseat of Dad's shiny black Buick. As Dad drove, I would spend my time looking out the back window and running my fingers through the white fur located in the back window. The fur had a pleasant vanilla-baked smell to it. Dad said it smelled that way because the sun warmed the vanilla scent on the paper tree that he had bought and tucked into the corner of the window. I didn't know or care that the fur in the window was fake. It was my daddy's and my daddy loved me; and right at that moment, I was with my daddy, so all was right with me.

Dad allowed me to visit his church with him on a few occasions. He attended Tindley Temple United Methodist Church, and I loved going there with him. I enjoyed the singing and the music. Sometimes the kids received cookies and juice after Sunday school, and while we were learning about Jesus, His love, and His protection, we would enjoy a sweet treat. As I grew, those lessons about Jesus would come to mean more than just sweet treats.

A few weeks after I learned about Jesus and His protection at Dad's church, my dad gave me a special birthday present. Dad bought me a square recorder to play vinyl 45-rpm records on. The one 45-record that Dad bought me was titled "Jesus, Be a Fence All Around Me." I played that 45 and sang that song so much. I loved that song so, so much.

Sometimes I would dream about Jesus coming to help me. At times, I would see a fence protecting me from the mean foster parents and their children. Other times I would dream that Jesus put a fence between me and the epilepsy spells I had. Then there were the times that I would ask Him to protect me from the kids at school who made fun of me and called me a monster. But the best times were when I would see Jesus, and at least it seemed that the things that were so hard would become easier—things like being hungry, or when foster parents and their children would take all that we had and leave us with almost nothing.

I loved that song and would sing it in my heart even when the 45 was put away. I would always dream that Jesus was going to come and take me away from all the sadness and put me in a better, happier place. Sometimes Jesus would help me by making me feel more joyous; other times Jesus would send my daddy to rescue me.

My dad did a lot for me and always included my siblings, Joyce and DeWitt, who were also in the foster care system. We were together a lot in foster placements, but then the agency began to separate us. My dad was always ready to help me when I needed him, and it was a joy spending time with him. My dad would always take on his responsibility, at least in my heart, by bringing money and candy and gifts to me, even when I was in those foster placements.

The following are events when my dad rescued my sister Joyce and me from extreme situations that had taken place at these particular houses. I had Dad's phone number and would call him when I needed him.

On one occasion, I somehow got a sore on my scalp, and the foster mom cut all my hair off. She never took me to a doctor to check on my condition; she just scalped me and sent me to school with a bald head. Joyce tried to put a scarf on my head to cover it, but the kids still laughed at me until my hair began to grow back. It was horrible at that house.

One day I was crying uncontrollably because something terrible had happened at this particular home. At times, Joyce and I slept in the same bed, since we were real sisters. Although Joyce was older than I was, she wet the bed a lot and was beaten for it. Joyce would sometimes tell the foster mom that I had wet the bed, not her. Even though I was dry and Joyce was wet, the foster mom would still beat me. One time the mom of the house threw Joyce's wet sheets into her face and told her to suck the sheets dry. Joyce was trembling as she put the sheets into her mouth, and with tears streaming down her face, she began to suck on the sheets.

That foster mom got so mad that she tied Joyce to the pillar of the rounding staircase and beat her on her back until her back began to bleed. Joyce was screaming and crying. I was screaming and crying, and I felt so helpless that I couldn't do anything to help her. I was so scared. Joyce still carries the scars from that beating on her back to this day. I didn't know what else to do. I called my dad at his candy store.

My, oh, my! My dad showed up at that house and kicked the door down. The foster mother was screaming, "I'm gonna call the police. You can't take these children!"

My dad said, "Paulette and Joyce, let's go!" He told the foster mother, "Call the police, because you are in trouble for what you have done to these children."

My dad put us in his shiny black Buick and took us to where our mom was living at that time. When we got there, I rang the bell, and Mom looked out the window. My dad yelled, my mom's nickname "Zeke, I got the girls. You need to call that agency and tell them what that lady has done to them." We stayed at Mom's house that night. In the morning, Mom called the agency, and I could hear her cussing and fussing about what had happened to us.

We did not go back to that house again. I remember being in court about the incidents that had occurred there. They asked me about Joyce's back and told me to tell them what I had seen. I eagerly told them what that foster mom had done to us. The foster mom said in court, "Well now, you know, Paulette is sickly. She has epileptic seizures and sometimes gets things mixed up. Also, placement is difficult for Paulette because of this epilepsy, but I was willing to care for her."

The foster mother thought she could hide behind my epileptic episodes and that nobody else would want to keep me after the seizures manifested. But I yelled out, "Yes, I do have epilepsy, but I know what you did to us." We never knew what happened to the foster mother of that home, but we never went back to that house.

In another house, the mom had locks on everything: the refrigerator, the phone, cabinets, and anything else that could have a lock. Although this house had many, many locks, it was not unusual for a foster home to have things locked up. We just came to expect it wherever we went. But at this house, we were never allowed to eat anything after we had eaten dinner. We were never allowed to get seconds on dinner either. This foster mother would lock up everything.

There were also several other children at this house. We were always hungry because she fed us only small amounts of food, and we couldn't get anything else because of the locks. We had to wait until the next meal for more to eat. Our stomachs ached because of hunger, but we thought we had figured out a way to get around her and her locks. We would sneak to the bathroom sink and drink water from the spigot because she had not put a lock on the sink. Ha, ha, ha—no locks on the sink!

When we got home from school at this house, we had to change our clothes. We would have to repeat-wear our clothes for two or three days in a row. I would sneak clothes out of the house to take to school and change into because of having to repeat-wear our clothes. I was sailing along fine until one of the other foster children got mad at me about something and told the foster mother. The foster mom beat me for doing that; I was scared to do it again, so I suffered through the teasing from the kids at school.

One particular girl at this foster home was a troublemaker. There were a lot of these types throughout foster land. These kids always did a lot of mean things to the other kids in the homes. One time we were all eating when the troublemaker at this house poured water under the chair of a girl who had a special set of problems. The aggressive girl then alerted the foster mom that the girl with special problems had wet herself. The girl that was lied about got slapped around and in trouble for the wetting episode. We could tell the difference between urine and water. Why couldn't this foster parent? There were so many things I did not understand in the foster system.

The little girl who was the victim was always so sad. She never smiled or laughed. This young girl had a sickness that caused brown and white spots to appear on her skin. She also acted different from the rest of us kids. Some of the boys would tease her and call her mentally retarded. Sometimes I would try to help the girl and tell the foster mother, "She didn't wet herself. One of the other kids poured water under her seat." That foster mom did not care. Those parents were so mean. Why did they have us anyway? The foster fathers lived there in the homes, but usually they were silent partners and the mothers were always in control of everything.

Dad had to rescue me from this house too. On one occasion, my dad brought me a large candy jar filled with lots of different coins. I was excited when I went to the door and saw that it was my dad and that he had something for me. He showed me the jar with all the coins. I was really excited. He said to make sure I shared with the other children in the home.

The foster mother reached for the jar of coins and said, "Thank you. Paulette can use this to buy things for school and any other little things she might need." My dad said, "Okay," and gave her the jar of coins. I wasn't disappointed when Dad gave the foster mother the jar because I thought she was going to oversee the money, like she said.

When the door shut and my dad got into his black Buick and pulled away from the house, something happened to my jar of coins. The foster mom took my jar and put it down her bosom. I would sometimes ask her for money from the jar that my dad had brought. She told me one time, "You have a dad." She was speaking about her husband and in not so many words telling me that I didn't have my own dad, Mr. William James Geiger. I used to cry at night about my jar—not only about the coins, but because Dad, my dad, had given it to me, and it was a way of being close to him and his love.

One of the other foster girls said one day, "Why don't you call your dad and tell him about your jar?" I was scared, and also the mother always had locks on the phone. This girl said she had noticed that one of the phones in the dining room did not have a lock on it, when we would come home from school. So a plan was put into motion. I came home from school one day and went right to the dining room phone and quickly dialed Dad's number.

My dad answered. I told him, "Daddy, I have not gotten any money from the jar yet, and I hate it here. There are locks on everything, including the phone and refrigerator, and I'm always hungry because we don't get enough to eat."

My dad was very upset. He said, "Be on the porch when I get there. I am coming right now." I don't know where the foster parents were, but I did not get caught on the phone. Jesus was being a fence all around me, just like in the song.

I did go out onto the porch and waited for my dad. Dad drove up to the house and got out of his car, talking very loudly. He was angry. The foster mother came running out onto the porch. Dad demanded,

"Where is the jar of money I gave you for my daughter, Paulette? My daughter said she has not received any of the coins out of the jar. Where is the jar?"

The foster mother reached down into her bosom and brought out the jar. Most of the coins were gone—only a few remained. I was shocked because I had kept asking her for coins all the time. My dad demanded, "What happened to Paulette's money?" The foster mother just looked at my dad. She had no response, no receipts, and nothing to say.

My dad said to me, "Get in the car." I ran to the car and got in. The foster mother started screaming at the top of her lungs: "He's taking my daughter! He's taking my daughter!" I did not pay much attention to the neighbors who had come out of their house and were listening and looking as my dad and I drove off in his shiny car.

Dad took me to my mother's apartment again. He was complaining, "Zeke, where do they find these foster parents?" In the same breath, he was telling my mom, "Call Mrs. Watson at the agency."

I stayed at Mom's, but the stay was not long. When Mrs. Watson came to pick me up, she and Mom talked. I hoped, as always, that they were talking about me staying with my mom. Not so. Whatever the conversation, whenever they finished and we were being taken away from Mom, she would always say, "They won't let me keep y'all, but I will be coming for my visits." This time, once again, I got into the car and waved good-bye to my mom as she looked from her second-floor apartment window.

I could never understand in my heart why I couldn't stay with either my mom or my dad, but each time I was able to call my dad and tell him that I was being treated poorly, he would come and rescue me. Sometimes when Dad couldn't come to take me away, he would say, "I'm going to call your mom and have you moved." Every time I called Dad, if he could come to get me, he would always take me back to Mom.

From Mom's house, we always went to a different foster home. Going to a new foster house always brought the wiggly feelings. I was never sure whether these new people were going to be nice, bad, or worse than where I had just come from. As we drove away, I thought about the times of our visits with Mom. Visits were always at the agency. During these visits, we would talk and play with the toys and games that were there for everyone. Sometimes we would get to see our siblings at these visits if it could be arranged in time. The agency would also provide snacks at these visits. The snacks were always good, because we never got enough food at the foster placements.

Years later as an adult, I was told by the agency that Dad had wanted to take me out of the system and care for me, but my mom was always at odds about it, though she never told them why. I could have been living with my dad from way back. I also found out from my mom's adult friends that my mom wanted us to come home many times, but she had to meet all of the requirements in order for that to happen. The agency required that we live in a house that could provide a bedroom for the girls and a separate bedroom for the boys, as well as a bedroom for Mom. Those requirements seemed simple enough; however, Mom had just been released from Muncy Prison.

I must say Mom worked very hard, and DeWitt, Joyce, and I were eventually all back home with Mom. We were all so delighted. We were all home with Mom! DeWitt and Joyce were released from foster care a little earlier than I was. I was about thirteen when I was allowed to go home to Mom. After Marcia and Michael, a younger sister and brother were born, we were a big, happy family living together. It was always better to be at home with Mom and my brothers and sisters than to be anywhere in the Philadelphia children's system.

SMILING ANGEL

I was having a lot of seizures one particular year, and as a result, I was being moved around to many different foster homes. My case worker told me that some parents did not like to see me sick so much and were not able to keep me. In my young mind, I thought they wanted only *normal* children, not someone who looked like she turned into a monster.

As we pulled up to yet another foster house, my eyes began to look all around the place. I was checking out the steps and the porch. I looked to see if there was furniture on the porch and if there was a backyard. My mind always raced as I began another new placement. As the case worker was parking, I began to think to myself, *Am I going to like it here? Are they going to like me? Are there other children here? What will happen when I have a seizure?* I experienced as much fear in leaving a home as I did in going to a new one. The unknown was quite powerful and gripping.

The foster parents came to the door to greet us, and the case worker made all the introductions. Everyone was smiling, and I wondered if this was all real, or was it going to turn out to be another bomb waiting to explode in my face? I heard other children in the house and thought, *Good, I am not going to be alone.*

I was taken to my bedroom and met the girl whom I would be sharing the room with. There were probably three or four children in that home, counting me. We all got along well. The foster parents were strict. I don't remember watching TV a lot in this home. We mostly stayed in our rooms playing made-up games with each other.

During dinnertime, the foster mother would say to us, "I talked to my mom today. You know, she can see you from her house when you walk home from school. She will let me know if you have been misbehaving."

One of the boys staying at the home at that time was named Tommy. He was older than the rest of us and always treated us like we were his little sisters. When necessary, he would take up for us and protect us at school and as we walked home. One day Tommy got into a fight. He was probably looking out for one of us, his little sisters. Nobody said anything about the fight when we got home. When we all sat down together to eat dinner, the foster mother said, "Mom told me you were in a fight today at school." We were all shocked! Tommy was hoping that she would not know anything about it, but it was too late—she already knew.

Several weeks later, we found out some strange information about our foster mother. Her mom, whom we thought was alive, was really *dead*. Somehow Tommy found out. He never told us how he found this out, but strange things began to happen. The foster mother started calling out to her mom, inviting her to come down the steps and join us for dinner. It was really spooky. All of us children knew that no one else lived in that house with us and that no one had come by for a visit. It seemed like the foster mother was going off the deep end. We all were scared.

Tommy told the case worker all about what was going on in that house. He told her about the foster mother calling her mother down to dinner and about her mother watching us walk home from school.

The case worker told Tommy not to worry about what was going on because she would check in to it. From then on, we kids stayed as close together as possible while we were in that home.

As usual, my seizures began to increase. They would just come over me, and usually right after that things would change. I felt I would be punished for being sick. The foster mom would cope with my seizures by sending me to my room when they were over. Since the seizures had increased and could become so violently disruptive, she gave me my own room. I could have a seizure at any time of day or night and in any season of the year. Having a seizure in the daytime when the weather was nice was really hard. I could hear all the other children in the neighborhood outside laughing and playing games. When we played outside, we enjoyed games like dodgeball, jacks, hide-and-seek, Mother May I, and a lot of other outdoor games.

After I had a seizure, I wasn't allowed to play. I was sent to my room to lie down. I would just lie there on the narrow bed, staring at the ceiling or inventing games. I wasn't having a seizure, but the mom would not let me get up. Sometimes I cried and wished I could be outside; at times, I cried myself to sleep. Other times, I just lay there wide awake.

One of the games I invented was to give names to all my ten fingers. Then my fingers would have conversations with one another, talking about all the things that were taking place in their lives. The finger families had no secrets. They shared everything with one another. This was probably one of the ways I found to cope with the horrific experiences I had to endure as a child. One day I shared the secret of my finger families with my case worker, and she only said that it was nice.

One particular evening I was sent to my room to lie down. I began to cry and rub my eyes. As I was rubbing my eyes, I moved my hands away from my eyes and saw a little light on the wall that had not been there before. The light started getting bigger and bigger, kind of like the good witch Glinda from *The Wizard of Oz*. I sat up on the side of the bed and asked, "What is that?" I was a little scared, but no sooner had the words come out of my mouth and the fear was about to creep in when—*poof*—that little light turned into a full-blown angel!

I knew it was an angel because she looked just like the ones I had seen in books. She had very large wings and was very beautiful. Her clothes were very fancy, and she never said a word. She did not have a wand or pixie dust; she just smiled at me. For some reason, I was no longer afraid. This angel kept looking at me and smiling. It seemed like she stayed with me for a long while, but it was only for a short time, and then she disappeared. I lay back down and went right to sleep.

The next morning, I could not wait to go downstairs and tell the foster mother what I had seen in my room. I told her all about the story, and all she could say was, "You did not see an angel in this house." I kept saying, "I did see her. I did see an angel—right there on the wall in my room." The foster mom would not hear of it. She just made me stop saying it.

Every time after that, whenever I was sent to my room, I would look at the blank wall, hoping to see my friend the angel. I would rub my eyes and look at the spot where she had appeared and then rub my eyes again to look for her, but she never came back. I guess she was just watching over me, even though I did not see her. Maybe she was my guardian angel.

For once, a case worker came through on her word for what we kids needed. The case worker that Tommy had talked to about the foster mother's mom came and did another visit. It didn't happen right away, but one by one, we were all removed from that home. We were all split up, and I never saw Tommy or any of the other children from that home again.

THE PARTY HOUSE

After number twenty, I lost count of the number of foster homes I had been in. Tragically, I experienced abuse on every level that no child should ever have to experience. While in this particular house, I had the absolute worst experience and suffering.

The story was always the same when it came time to move. The case worker would say, "Well, Paulette, that family tried, but they can no longer help you." I knew it was all about my epilepsy. I was shifted from home to home to home. No kid should ever have to go through all that.

Well, here we were, off to a new place. My case worker had said that I should like it at this house because the foster parents were a little younger than the parents at some of the other homes I had lived in. This family also had a son my age, and we would probably be in the same grade at school, since we were both nine years old at that time.

The case worker pulled her car up to the house, and both Mr. and Mrs. Harrison met us at the door. They were both fashionably dressed. I'm not sure why, but I noticed that Mr. Harrison had on dress pants and a very nice shirt. Mrs. Harrison had on a very pretty dress with flashy earrings, bracelets, and high heels. It was unusual to see foster parents dressed like that. They looked different from other foster parents. They did not look like the typical stay-at-home foster parents.

We sat in the living room and did the regular introductions. Mrs. Harrison introduced her younger son and stated that they also had an older, grown son. After a brief visit, the case worker said her good-byes and assured us that she would be visiting again at a later time. Once again, I was in a new home, facing new people, new fears, and new challenges.

This placement was in a very big house with three floors. All the rooms in this house were very large, even the bedrooms. The new foster mom took me on a tour of the house. It was so big I thought I might get lost in it. She took me upstairs to the second floor and showed me where my room was. There were other bedrooms on this floor as well. I don't know who slept in those other bedrooms, and I don't think there were any other foster kids in that house. Mrs. Harrison did not take me up to the third floor.

When Mrs. Harrison and I got back downstairs, the foster dad, Mr. Harrison, turned on some music. Mrs. Harrison began to prepare dinner. I had heard that type of music before. Mr. Harrison was playing songs by Marvin Gaye and other artists from the 1960s. While dinner was cooking, the family was dancing and singing out loud along with the music. They were smiling at each other and laughing together. I just stood there and watched them. I thought, *This seems like it is going to be a fun family.*

The Harrisons always had a lot of parties in their house on the weekends. Many people would come over to their house; you could hear music and laughter, and the smell of good food was in the air. The foster mom would let me stay at the party for just a little while. Soon enough, I would be sent upstairs to my room to go to bed or play in my room. Mostly she would just tell me, "It's time for you to go to bed." My bed was like a large crib with pull-up bars on both sides. She told me they had to use this type of bed because of my seizures and that she did not want me to fall out of the bed during the night and get hurt. I had never seen a bed like that before for someone who was not a baby.

For some strange reason, while staying at this house, I would frequently get a fever. Mrs. Harrison would always give me medicine to break the fever, and sometimes I would doze off to sleep. Before dozing off, I would hear the laughter and music and voices from downstairs. It seemed like everyone was having a good time. The Harrisons' younger son was always allowed to stay up and join in with the party. I thought she was afraid that I would have a seizure in front of her party friends and scare them, since people said I turned into a monster when I had a seizure. Maybe that is why she put me to bed, but not her son.

One night she did her regular routine. They were having a party with good food, lots of friends, jumping music, and lots of laughter, but off to bed I went. I was so sad. Sometimes I would cry because I did not want to go to bed so early. But you learned early in those homes to do whatever the foster mom or dad said; you had no say in the matter.

This particular night, the grown son came down to my room. I didn't see him often because he had a job and left home early every day. When he entered my room, he put his hand over my mouth and said, "Shhh," to quiet me. He scared me, coming into my room like that, because he had always been pleasant the few times that I had seen him in the home. He picked me up out of my bed and took me upstairs to the third floor to his room. I didn't know what he was going to do. I wondered why he wasn't at the party, since that is where all the fun was going on.

He laid me on his bed and put thick tape over my mouth and around my hands. My eyes got big, and I started to cry. I was screaming, but no one could hear me because of the tape over my mouth. I was scooting, trying to get off the bed and run out of his room, but he was too quick for me and was much bigger than I was. He slammed me back onto the bed on my stomach and pushed my face down hard onto the bed to help muffle my screams.

I didn't know what he was doing. I didn't know why he was doing this to me. I could hear the music from the party going on downstairs, even though we were on the third floor, but I could not hear the voices clearly like from my room on the second floor.

My thoughts began to swirl: *Why isn't he at the party? Why is this happening to me? This is worse than any seizure I have ever had. Where is my mother? Where is my daddy? How can I get my daddy to come and rescue me? Why won't somebody come and make him stop hurting me?* The whole time I was screaming and crying, but no one ever knew it.

Afterwards, he picked me up and carried me back to my room on the second floor and put me back into my bed. He took the tape off my hands and mouth and said, "Shhh," as a reminder. Then he told me not to say anything to anyone about it, because if I did, his parents would get in trouble, and it would be entirely my fault.

I didn't know what had happened to me, but I knew I was too scared to say anything. I was filled with fear about all of what had happened, but also, I didn't even know what to call this thing that had happened to me! I was taken up to the third floor by this oldest son many, many times. Each time he treated me the same brutal way.

He would tape my mouth and hands and warn me not to tell, or his family would be in trouble. I am not sure how long this went on.

Once back in my bed, I would cry myself to sleep. But there were just more tears. I cried a lot. There was so much to cry about. My thoughts pounded in my head: *I have lost so much. So much has been taken from me. So many people have abused me. So many people have mistreated me. Where is my mom? My mother doesn't want me. Where is my dad? My dad doesn't want me. The Women's Christian Alliance can't find anyone who wants me. Why? Why? Why? Why did all of this have to happen to me? Does this happen to all little girls or just little girls who have seizures?*

I must have had a seizure during one of those weekend parties and was taken to my room. When I came out of the seizure, I remember that I was holding on to the foster mom and did not want her to go back downstairs and leave me. Mrs. Harrison told me that I would be all right, since the seizure was over, but that she would send her youngest son to check on me from time to time.

I couldn't tell anybody what was happening to me, so I talked about it with my finger families. That was a strange little game I had created, but I would cry for all the families and laugh at all the good things that happened in the finger families. It always seemed that the good stuff happened only once in a great while.

One night the oldest son snatched me from my bed, as was his custom, and took me upstairs to his room. The music from the party was loud, and everyone downstairs was laughing and having a good time. I remember crying through the tape and tears rolling down my cheeks. As I lay there, my body was being violated. I was hurting, scared, and screaming through the tape, but I happened to turn my head toward the door. Standing there in the doorway was the younger son. He stood there looking at me. He had a look of shock and disbelief on his face. But he never said a word and left very quietly. The older brother never saw him. When the older Harrison brother finished, he returned me to my bed as usual, took the tape off my mouth and hands, and warned me not to get his family into trouble.

I wondered about the younger Harrison son. Why didn't he say something while he was standing there? What did he do after he left the doorway? Why was he on the third floor with the party going on? Had his mother sent him to check on me because of my seizures? When he did not see me in my bed, had he gone to look for me? Is that why he was on the third floor? Was he coming to the third floor to alert his brother that he could not find me, that I was missing from my bed? What did he tell his mother when he went back down to the party? Did I get the Harrison family in trouble by letting the older son do that to me? Would I have to leave the Harrison house? Leaving this pain and torment would not be all bad, but what would I face somewhere else?

I don't know what the younger Harrison son said about what he saw, but a few days later, Mrs. Harrison told me that the case worker was coming to take me to another foster home. I asked her, "Why do I have to leave?" She just said something about they could not take care of me any longer, and with the seizures, it was not working out. She seemed sad. I felt sad and scared and excited all in one, because once again I was leaving the familiar and going to the unknown. I was dealing with fear on top of fear. When you are on the outside looking in, you think that a family is going to be kind and friendly and loving. At least, that's what you see on the TV commercials. But real life outside of the TV was *drama* day after day after day.

I wondered if the younger son told his parents what he had witnessed and they then got me out of there as fast as they could. Everything about that situation was kept hush-hush, because the case worker never said anything about the older son and what he had done to me.

As an adult, I returned to Philadelphia for a visit. My firstborn daughter made the trip with me, and we were enjoying spending time with family and friends. On one of those days I visited co-workers at John Wanamaker's department store. I had started working at Wanamaker's in my senior year of high school. They were so pleased with my performance that they told me I had a job guaranteed every summer that I came home from college. I kept in touch with the friends I had made at Wanamaker's, and I was proud to share pictures of my husband and baby. We had enjoyed a great visit that day, and this was shaping into a great trip.

After leaving Wanamaker's, I was standing at the bus stop to take the public bus back to Granny's house. We had begun to call Momma Liz "Granny" back in my teenage years. When the bus arrived, I stepped onto the bus, hoping to find a seat nearby to settle down for the ride.

I was shocked and my heart riveted when I looked into the bus driver's eyes. This bus operator, this person out in the public sector, accessible to children and other unsuspecting people, was the man who, when I was a child, had snatched me from my bed, bound my hands together and taped my mouth, and violated my body without mercy until the agency sent me away from the "party house."

I said, "Hello, Mr. Harrison."

He said, "Hi. Do you know me?"

I said, "Yes, your parents used to take care of me. How are they?"

He said, "They are fine. How are you?"

I responded, "I am married and live in Pittsburgh, and we have a little girl."

He said nothing else. As I continued to a seat, I wondered what he was thinking. I know what I was thinking. My mind flashed back to the horror of those occasions when he had total disregard for me as a child, as a person, or even as someone vulnerable and needing care and compassion. I wanted to yell out to the people on the bus that this driver was a sex molester, someone who should be locked up and not allowed around other people. But thank God for the counseling I had received through the years. Thank God that the Spirit of God rose up in me, and I knew I had victory over this tragic part of my life. Thank God, forgiveness prevailed!

As I stepped off the bus, I said, "Tell your mother I said hello, and God bless you, Mr. Harrison." I could only hope that God would deal with him for what he had done to me and who knows if to others as well. I, however, was able to step off that bus and go forward. With freedom in my spirit, I was able to continually do the work of the Lord. "If the Son therefore shall make you free, ye shall be free indeed" (John 8:36).

OUT OF FOSTER CARE—
HOME WITH MOM

BUS RIDE TO HARRISBURG, PENNSYLVANIA

S ummertime—finally! School was out for the summer. Day after day, we had gotten up early, eaten breakfast quickly, and started out on the long walk to school. We endured long, boring school days and then made the long walk back home. But now, now all of that was over. These were the long days of summer.

Summer meant *fun*, especially when we were with Mom. We were all living at home with Mom at that time, and she would allow us to stay up late, playing outside right in front of the building. We could sleep until noon if we wanted. We loved summertime. But this morning was different.

It was early on this summer morning when our mother woke us up. Things seemed a bit strange on that day. Mom was dressed in new clothes and smelled of her favorite perfume. She was speaking in excited tones. Marcia and Michael spotted new outfits and slapped each other a high-five in celebration. Mom had also placed a new outfit on the dresser for me. It was always fun to get new clothes, but I sensed that something else was going on.

Mom hurried us along, stating that we were going to Harrisburg to meet our step-grandfather and our older sister, and if we had time, we would also visit our older brother, DeWitt, who was in the same area. We had to eat quickly because we had to take a hack to get downtown. Taxicabs didn't usually come to our neighborhood, but we still had transportation to get where we needed to go.

We were excited about many things that day. We were wearing new clothes, we were leaving our neighborhood, and we were going to meet someone new, our step-grandfather. This was all pretty exciting to us kids. We were going into places unknown. All we had ever known was South Philadelphia. We hadn't seen our sister, Joyce, in a long time, as she drifted in and out of our home frequently, so we were happy that we would be seeing her again.

As usual, the youngest took the longest to eat and get dressed, so we had to rush in order to get downtown on time. We were all excited and thought we were looking good all dressed up in our new clothes. We piled into the hack and sped off to the Greyhound bus station downtown. Mom was grateful that the driver got us to town quickly.

We kids were enjoying the difference in our summer routine. We got out of the hack and heard and saw all the sights and sounds of the big city of Philadelphia. Still rushing, we hurried inside the Greyhound bus station. We boarded a bus labeled "Harrisburg, Pennsylvania" and settled into our seats. We had never been to Harrisburg. This was going to be an exciting summer. We would have something different and new to say at show-and-tell when school started.

After we got situated on the Greyhound, the ride seemed to last forever, although the distance from Philadelphia to Harrisburg was only two hours. My sister and brother invented games to entertain themselves during the ride and were concerned about keeping their new clothes from getting wrinkled. I watched my mom during that ride and noticed that her expression seemed very determined. I was only about thirteen years old at that time, but I had learned to read my mom's expressions quickly, since I had often been separated from her throughout my young life.

As this was our first trip out of Philadelphia, there was much for our young eyes to see while the bus traveled the countryside heading west. We were able to see the Schuylkill River for a short distance of the trip, and then nothing but small towns. The weather was good, and out of the bus windows, we saw farms and the usual animals: cows, sheep, and chickens. One thing we noticed once we left Philadelphia was that the wide-open green spaces were a stark contrast to the crowded concrete city we lived in. But I was more interested in what my mom was thinking and planning.

Mom did not give us any information as to who our step-grandfather was. She said we would find out when we met him. Then Mom said something very strange. She said, "You will meet your older sister today." Something didn't add up. What could possibly be going on? We had already met our older sister, Joyce. What could Mom mean by that statement? Marcia and Michael were too busy enjoying the view from the window to be concerned about what Mom had just said. However, Mom knew I was looking at her for answers, although I knew better than to ask about "grown-folks' business."

Finally, Mom said, "Your step-grandfather's name is Mr. William Brown, and your older sister's name is Madelyn Carol Britton." I continued to search Mom's face for answers, but she just continued to look determined. Mom said no more about the matter for the remainder of the ride. I knew there had to be more to that story.

Even from an early age, I always wanted to know stuff — give me the details! But I also knew to just wait.

As soon as we got off the bus, my brother and sister began to ask Mom about eating, but I was interested in the sights of this new city. We had never been to Harrisburg before. I wondered about these new people and how they lived. After lunch, we took a taxi to the suburb of Oberlin, a quiet part of the city. The houses were large with big porches and wide front and back yards. Trees lined both sides of the streets. Mom paid the taxi driver as we stood on the sidewalk, looking up at the big brown house.

As Mom knocked on the door of the house, Marcia and Michael sat on the porch swing, dangling their legs and enjoying the suspended feeling. An older man with a broad smile opened the door. This man spoke kindly to Mom and gave her a big hug, almost picking her up off the porch. I was standing at Mom's side, and Marcia and Michael joined us, trying to see what all the commotion was about. We watched silently as Mom semi-relaxed as the gentle man almost sheltered her. He said, "Come in, come in." We hesitated, but Mom said, "Paulette, Marcia, Michael, this is Mr. William Brown, your step-grandfather." We spoke politely and entered the house behind Mom. Mom and Mr. Brown chatted as he led us all to the front room of the house. Mom asked "Stepdad," as she called him, how he was and about other family matters.

We learned that Mr. Brown had married our grandmother, Pauline Virginia Hurst. Grandma Pauline and Mr. Brown married when our mom was about eighteen months old. Mr. Brown was the only father our mother had ever known, but she rarely talked about her younger years. Actually, Mom never told us much about Grandma Pauline or Mr. Brown. We basically knew of our grandparents in name only.

When we met Mr. Brown, he seemed glad to see Mom and to meet us. To us, he was an older man, probably in his sixties, and we called him Mr. Brown. Oberlin was a very small suburb. The area looked more like the country than it did a city.

The conversation and time spent with Mr. Brown was brief. We didn't understand why we did not stay with him for long, but we were on an adventure, and we wanted to experience all that Mom was going to present to us on that day. Mom told Mr. Brown that we were going to visit Madelyn Carol. Marcia and Michael were fidgeting when Mom said that, and I just waited to hear more. My heart skipped a beat. *Who is this person?* I wondered.

Nothing more was said about Madelyn Carol at that time. I didn't know until that day that we had another sister. Mom went on to tell Mr. Brown that all her children had been given French names. Mom proudly told Mr. Brown the names of all her children: Madelyn Carol, DeWitt, Joyce, Paulette, Marcia, and Michael. Mr. Brown called us a taxi, and the address we were delivered to was located in the public-city housing area.

Madelyn Carol lived on the top floor of the Harrisburg city projects with her husband and three small children. Her husband was not at home on that visit. Two of the children had on nothing but diapers, probably because it was so hot that summer.

Mom spoke kindly to Madelyn Carol, but Madelyn Carol's response was cool and guarded. Mom spoke to Madelyn Carol's children, saying, "Hello, children. Come to your grandmother."

The children were running towards my mom, excitedly playing. But Madelyn Carol got very angry and said, "You are not their grandmother—my mother is! And better yet, nobody calls me Madelyn Carol. My name is *Carol*!" That angry outburst certainly raised questions in my inquisitive mind, but I said nothing. I just listened, hoping more details would spill out.

Mom didn't defend her statement about the kids being her grandchildren, nor did she give explanation to Carol's statement about her mother. Mom expected that Carol would be bitter, hurt, and confused about having been given away as a child. Mom allowed Carol to experience her pain and anger, but unfortunately, she was unable to comfort Carol through those feelings.

Mom just continued playing with her grandchildren and said, "Carol, what are the children's names?"

Grudgingly, Carol responded, stating, "Lionel, Robin, and Susan." Each child beamed as their mother spoke their name. Mom told the children our names and said that we were their relatives, their young aunts and an uncle. Mom was enjoying herself with her grandchildren, despite what Carol had said. The children themselves were enjoying these new visitors. They didn't care if this lady with these visiting kids was another grandmother or not. They were having fun.

Carol finally pleaded, "You have to leave. My husband is coming home soon, and he does not know anything about you or about me being adopted."

Mom said to Carol, "Okay. I just wanted to see you and my grandchildren. I also wanted you to meet some of your sisters and one of your brothers." Mom was having a difficult time separating from her grandchildren, so we stayed there a long time. It would not become clear to me who Carol's mother was until some time later.

We had stayed too long at Carol's house, so there was not enough time to visit DeWitt. DeWitt was incarcerated at the Camp Hill State Prison. A visit to DeWitt would have to take place on another trip. That was exciting. That meant there would be another trip. Hopefully, we would have that other trip in this same summer. Boy, show-and-tell was really going to be fun for us next school year!

Anyway, we had to hurry and get back to the bus station to catch the Greyhound back to Philadelphia. We were all very quiet during the bus ride home. I could tell that Mom was thinking about the roll-er-coaster events of the day. She was very sad, and tears streamed down her face as we silently returned to our neighborhood.

A couple of months later, Mom took me with her to the prison at Camp Hill to visit DeWitt. After we got off the Greyhound bus, we had a very long walk around a very long and high wall to get to the entrance of the prison. After having our bodies and our bags checked by the guards, we had to settle for lunch from the vending machines. We took a picture with DeWitt, but we had to buy a ticket from the guard, and an inmate then took our photo together.

The visit with DeWitt was good. He made us laugh, telling us stories about his cutting inmates' hair in prison. DeWitt liked to sing, and of course he sang for his mother. Way too soon our long-awaited, brief visit with DeWitt was over. Alarm bells were ringing; loudspeakers were informing us that visiting hours were now ended; and guards were telling us that we now had to leave. I was sad to leave DeWitt, but Mom had a few tears in her eyes and was sighing heavily. We retraced the long walk from the prison entrance around the long, high wall back to the bus stop and returned to South-West Philadelphia. We did not stop to visit with Mr. Brown or with Carol and her family on that visit.

I lost contact with my dad after leaving foster placement. I lost his phone number. My mom moved around a lot, and so did my dad. Mom never let me go down to South Street to see if the candy store was still there.

Shortly after our visit with my brother DeWitt, mom told Marcia and Michael and me that we were moving to South Philadelphia. Joyce was older than we were, and she often stayed elsewhere, but would come and see us. When we moved to South Philadelphia, we happened to move across the street from the Marion Anderson Recreation Center. We lived in a third-floor apartment, and we were happy to be together. We enjoyed spending time at the center, playing on the playground, in the gym, and in the swimming pool. Summers were fun in the neighborhood at the center.

Jesus was still watching over me and somehow directing me. On one particular day, I happened to be walking home from school and decided to take the long way home instead of the shortcut. While walking through this different neighborhood, I noticed that these houses did not look the apartment buildings near our house. These houses had porches and yards.

I continued walking home, thinking I'd better hurry before Mom began to wonder where I was. I walked another block, and sitting on one of the porches was a man in a chair with his head down a little. The man somehow seemed familiar. My heart jumped just a little. I didn't want to get overexcited. But even before the words could form in my mouth, my heart told me that the man in the chair on the porch was my dad! I was so shocked and excited.

I ran up on the porch and said, "Daddy!" He seemed like he was asleep, and I think I may have scared him a little.

He looked up and said, "Paulette?" and I answered, "Yes!" I am sure I had grown quite a bit since he had last seen me, and I was about thirteen now. He reached out to me, and we hugged each other. I had found my dad. He had a lot of questions. He asked, "Where have you been? What are you doing down here in South Philly?"

I was just so overwhelmed that I had found my daddy. I was just smiling and smiling and trying to answer his questions. I said, "Mom and us just moved down here." I told him exactly where we had moved to. I continued to tell him, "I was taking the long way home from school, and that's when I saw you. Daddy, what happened? I haven't seen you in a long time, and I lost your phone number."

He hugged me again and said, "I went to the agency, asking where you were, and they said you had been released and were back home with your mother. I asked for your address, and Mrs. Watson said I had to wait for your mother to contact me with that information. I never heard anything from Zeke, so I just hoped that I might run into you and your mother somewhere. Plus, I have been sick and was in the hospital for a while. I am so glad to see you!"

I said, "I am too, Daddy. I am going to stop back by tomorrow. I have to go now before Mom starts to wonder where I am." We hugged and kissed, and I ran the rest of the way home.

When I got home, Mom was not there, which was good for me. Marcia said, "Mom went to the store when I first got home."

I went up to my room, smiling. Just to think, my dad actually lived only a few blocks away from us. My heart was so happy. Warm memories and thoughts began to form in my head: *I will take the long way home after school each day so I can stop at Dad's house. It was so nice to see Dad again and talk to him.* Today had been comforting, and I felt loved for those brief moments spent with him. *I will just have to remember not to stay too long at Dad's, or Mom will wonder why it is taking me so long to get home from school.*

I could not wait until the bell rang for dismissal from school. Off to my dad's house I went. It was always a joy spending time with my dad. We talked about a lot of things, including school and my grades. Dad had a large sore on his leg, and it always had a bandage wrapped around it. When I asked Dad about the bandage, he said, "It's because of my sugar." I had no idea what that was. But because Dad said so, it was fine with me.

My dad would say strange things sometimes, but in a funny way— like the time he said, "You know, Paulette, I woke up in a morgue one day." Well, his joke was lost on me. I didn't know what a morgue was. Because of the lost look on my face, Dad explained his statement. Dad said that he must have gone into a sugar-induced coma and that everyone thought he was dead. The morgue is where they take anyone who has died. He said he woke up with a sheet over his face, and he started moaning really loudly. The nurse heard him and pulled back the sheet and started screaming. That room was the last place you would expect to find someone alive covered by a sheet. We laughed about it, but I am sure that it was not funny at the time.

I'm sure Mom knew I was stopping by Dad's house, but she never said anything about it or never told me not to go.

Some of the talks with my dad were serious. He told me that his mom had died the day that she gave birth to him. He never told me her name or where she was from. Wow, that was my grandmother. I wish I would have asked him about her. Now I will never know that part of my family.

One time Dad also told me, "Paulette, do you know that you have two brothers?"

"I do?" I asked.

Dad chuckled and said, "Yes."

"Who are they, and where are they?" I wanted to know.

Dad said they lived in Philadelphia near us, and if I came back to the house on Saturday, he would take me to meet them. I was so excited. I had more brothers. I was going to meet them on Saturday. I could hardly wait.

When I got home that day, I was so excited. I told my sister Marcia all about everything. I told her about finding my dad and seeing him after school each day and about meeting my two brothers. Marcia was excited for me, and she just smiled as she watched me tremble with excitement.

I'm not sure why my mom and dad were not together. We all knew that we had different fathers, and Mom had a habit of not putting our dads' names on our birth certificates. We never knew why our fathers were not named. Mom would just tell us who our father was, and all the fathers owned up to being our fathers. My older brother and older sisters may have been an exception to the fact and had a father's name listed on their birth certificates, but I was not sure. I met all the other fathers except theirs.

The day before that special Saturday arrived, Marcia and I were playing a card game. We got into a disagreement about the game, and Marcia was losing. We were playing the game 500, which we played a lot. She got mad and ran into the room where Mom was and told her all about my plans to meet my dad and brothers on Saturday.

Mom was not happy about Dad's and my plan. Saturday came, and Mom watched me like a hawk all day long. She had me doing lots and lots of chores, and I never could get out of the house on that Saturday. Marcia didn't say anything; she just watched me all day. I was so angry with her and my mom. I now wish that I had been a disobedient child and had just walked out of the house that day. I wish that I hadn't cared about the consequences. But I did.

I remained compliant and stayed in the house all that day. I was so sad in my heart. I didn't know when I would be able to meet my brothers, but I couldn't wait for school to get out on Monday so I could talk to Dad. Finally, the bell rang to end the school day. I bolted out of the school and was off to my dad's house.

I knocked on the door, and the landlady answered the door. She knew I was looking for my dad. The landlady said that my dad had gotten sick and been taken to the hospital. She did not think that he would be coming back to this house. I was so sad. Not only had I missed the opportunity to see my dad on Saturday and meet my two brothers, but now my dad was sick and in the hospital.

The landlady didn't tell me which hospital my dad was in. I guess she didn't want to say too much to a child. I did not tell anyone. My heart was broken. My heart sang, "Jesus, be a fence around Daddy" every day. About a week later, Mom told me that she had heard that James, my father, had died. I just looked at her in disbelief. Tears were building up in my eyes, and my heart was beating hard and fast. I was getting mad and didn't know what to do.

Although my mother had many issues to deal with in her life, and she was starting to get sick as well, she was not an unkind woman. But right then, I felt like she was being unkind. My mom just made that statement about my dad and walked away. She did nothing to console me and said nothing else about it. I didn't know anything about a funeral or a viewing or even what would happen next. My heart and head hurt so badly. Now I would never to get to meet my two brothers.

Now my dad was gone. He was gone. Who would make me smile like my dad had done? Who would be my hero? I would never again be able to see my dad, hear my dad's voice in joy and laughter. I would never again hear his voice in anger at what others were doing to me. I would never again hear my dad's voice in praise of my accomplishments. My life had already been built upon a Swiss cheese foundation, and it seemed that the holes were getting larger and larger and that I was just slipping through the openings. Mom never said anything else to me about my dad, whether dead or alive.

Even though Mom said she had heard that James had died, my heart was not ready to accept that as final. I never stopped looking for my dad, even if only in my heart. Some days I would concede to myself, *Dad must be deceased, because if he was still alive, with all our encounters with each other and knowing how much he loved me, I know he would have found me.* I have been unsuccessful in my search for my dad and brothers, but as I keep on searching, I will allow Father God to fill that position in my life.

Right after I was married, my husband and I moved to Pittsburgh, Pennsylvania. Our family was growing, and we had two children at the time. I contacted the Women's Christian Alliance agency, inquiring as to why and how I had been placed into their system. They responded with the letter below:

WOMEN'S CHRISTIAN ALLIANCE

P.O. BOX 2660 • 1610-16 North Broad Street • Philadelphia, Pennsylvania 19121

(215) 236-9911

ANN V. WHITE, MCSW
Executive Director

January 31, 1978

Mrs. Paulette Davidson
1754 Paul Court
Pittsburgh, Penna. 15221

Dear Paulette:

It was nice hearing from you again and I am responding to give you as much of the desired information as I can.

Unfortunately, our records don't contain any employment or social security data on your father. We can document the fact that he sustained visits with you with some degree of regularity from the time you entered the agency's care and, while he always expressed interest in gaining your custody, he and your mother were sharply at odds on this. She never explained her objections beyond saying her reasons were strictly personal. The real factor against your discharge to your father, however, was his failure to present us a definite plan for becoming directly responsible for you.

I can't account for the fact that you had not known before that your father's name was William as, throughout our records, he was alternately identified as William as well as James Geiger. Perhaps his full name was William James Geiger, or vice versa. The last address we had for him (in 1964) was 1710 Wallace Street. I have no idea how helpful this would be at this point in time as he had an established history of moving around a lot.

Our City Hall was unable to provide any identifying data and it may well be that your father was born elsewhere.

You and your brother and sister (Joyce and Dewitt) came into the agency's care on March 5th, 1954 because your mother had been sentenced to a prison term on a charge of larceny. According to her, she was innocent and had been framed by another young woman with whom she had been sharing an apartment. Whatever the case, she was sent to Muncy but paroled after a year and a half.

I am sorry I can't be of greater assistance but this was what I could extract from the old case records.

Good luck with your family. I am sure your own youngsters are source of both enjoyment and work.

Mrs. Ivia Benson and Mrs. Edna Hubbard send best wishes and love.

Sincerely yours,

(Miss) Ann V. White, MSW
Executive Director

United Way

AVW:lw

FOSTER-FAMILY CARE, COUNSELING AND ADOPTION

CHANGED

Mrs. Jennie Cobbs was also known as "Momma Jennie" by those close to her, including her church friends. Momma Jennie was the gracious lady who had allowed our mother, at a young age and fresh off the Greyhound bus, to rent the room in her house. Momma Jennie was Elizabeth Cobbs's mother. Elizabeth Cobbs was Mom's sister-friend, and we called her "Momma Liz," or "Granny," throughout our lives.

I was fresh out of the foster care system and was able to be back at home with Mom, and Marcia and Michael, my younger sister and brother. I was able to return home because Granny was helping Mom take care of us. Because Mom had help, the agency allowed us to all be together. Mom was doing the best that she could, although her health had begun to steadily decline.

While we were living with Mom, Momma Jennie would often take us to church with her, and we enjoyed going. At times, there would be a lot of us going to church together. Sometimes it would be Momma Jennie; her great-grandchildren, Michelle and Rhonda; my nieces, Vashti and Larniece; along with my siblings and me. We could all be seen trailing down the street to get the bus to go to church. Other times, Momma Jennie's other granddaughter would go to church with us. Her name was Paulette also. Since there were two of us named Paulette, they called her Big Paulette, and they called me Li'l Paulette.

Big Paulette was grown and married, but she still loved to go to church with us. Big Paulette was unable to have children of her own, so she was always claiming somebody's child. We all loved her. I believe if Big Paulette had still been living when I had my youngest child, she would have come to Pittsburgh and taken her. I named my youngest daughter after Big Paulette.

We kids were all happy to be going to church, and we couldn't wait to get there. We would all traipse down to the bus stop. Momma Jennie attended Miracle Temple Church in West Philadelphia. Rev. R. W. Schambach was the senior pastor, and Rev. Wiley T. Hill was the associate pastor of the church.

Of course, we were in church all day long. We would eat breakfast before we left, but we would get to church early on Sunday morning for Sunday school. We would stay for morning service. Sometimes after that, they held what was called afternoon service, and we would remain for that service, then attend night service. Church on Sunday was like going to work or school — it sometimes lasted all day long.

On the Sundays that we remained for afternoon service, Granny would give us teenagers money, and we would all walk together to the local fast-food restaurant. Other times, we would just get snacks from the neighborhood store between the services. Between afternoon and night services, sometimes Momma Jennie would be able to get a ride, and she would take the younger children home. Staying for night service was too tedious for the younger ones, but Momma Jennie would always come back for night service.

By the time Momma Jennie and I got home on Sunday nights, we were exhausted and dragging, but our hearts were happy. We had been with friends and family, we had enjoyed good fellowship, and we were able to watch the hand of God touch people's lives.

Momma Jennie was in her senior years, but you could never tell it. She was still working every day and taking the bus to work. I think somehow she was strengthened by the molasses water she would faithfully drink and the dark stuff inside the chicken bones that she would crack open and eat. I would look at the bones on her plate after she was done and say, "Momma Jennie, the dogs won't want them bones when you get finished with them."

She would just smile and say, "I reckon not."

Momma Jennie loved us and talked to us about Jesus all the time. She made sure we got to Sunday school every Sunday. Church was her life. I loved to stay up under Momma Jennie and loved to listen to her many talks. Momma Jennie always had something great to say, not only about the Bible, but different sayings and thoughts about life itself. She would say, "Li'l Paulette, it does not hurt to speak to people and say hi." Other times, she would just be thinking about Jesus and say, "Li'l Paulette, Jesus is my all and all." Then she would go into some type of story about her life or the Bible.

Since I was always hanging around under Momma Jennie's elbow, folks would say, "Li'l Paulette, you are going to be just like Momma Jennie—a little Momma Jennie."

One Sunday in March of 1967, after having a nice, hot homemade breakfast prepared by Granny, we children finished getting ready for church. Momma Jennie didn't eat breakfast; she just drank her molasses water. Off we all went to the bus stop, heading to Miracle Temple to start our Sunday event.

Momma Jennie watched as we each went to our Sunday school classes, and she greeted our teacher. Our teacher, Sister Stiff, waved and softly called out, "Morning, Momma Jennie."

This particular Sunday, our teacher asked us, "How many of you are a Christian?" I didn't exactly know what she was talking about, but everyone else raised their hands, so I raised mine too.

Sister Stiff started talking about Adam and Eve and how they had sinned against God. She told us that we were all sinners, including her, and that we needed Jesus. She taught us how Jesus had died on the cross and shed His blood for our sins. She said He showed us how much He loved us, and by shedding His blood, He took all our sins away. She explained it so clearly and to our level of understanding.

I was getting tears in my eyes, and some of the other children in my class were getting teary-eyed also. I did not know why then, but later on I found out that it was the Spirit of the Lord drawing me and the others to Christ: "No man can come to Me except the Father which hath sent Me draw him" (John 6:44).

Our teacher then said, "You can accept Jesus into your heart today. He loves you. Does anyone want to accept Jesus today?" We all raised our hands. She led us in what some call the traditional "sinner's prayer."

We repeated these words after Sister Stiff: "Dear Jesus, I am a sinner. Come into my heart, and wash me in Your blood. Take all my sins away. Thank You for dying on the cross for my sins and being my Lord and Savior. Amen."

Then she had prayer with us as a group. From that very day, I knew Jesus had come into my life and changed me. Because I was convinced at that early age that Jesus had changed me, when I heard the singer Tramaine Hawkins sing the song titled "Changed," I became very excited. The lyrics of that song spoke volumes in my life, then and now. The song declares that I am free, my sins are washed away, Jesus has made me whole, and He has changed my life. I probably now consider this song to be the theme song for my life.

You will never be the same again when Jesus comes into your life completely. You will look at your old life and say with joy, "I'm changed!"

MIRACLES STILL HAPPEN

Isaiah 53:5 reads, "But he was wounded for our transgressions, He was bruised for our iniquities: the chastisement of our peace was upon Him and with His stripes we are healed."

I felt that I was born with a demon spirit. Society and medical science diagnosed my condition as epilepsy. However, the Word of God originally classified epilepsy as a demon:

> And lo, a spirit taketh him and he suddenly crieth out; and it tcarcth him that he foameth again and bruising him hardly departeth from him. . . . And as he was yet a coming, the devil threw him down, and tare him. And Jesus rebuked the unclean spirit, and healed the child, and delivered him again to his father. Luke 9:39, 42 KJV

> And when they approached the multitude, a man came up to Him, kneeling before Him and saying, Lord, do pity and have mercy on my son, for he has *epilepsy* and he suffers terribly. . . . And Jesus rebuked the demon, and it came out of him, and the boy was cured instantly.Matthew 17:14–15, 18 AMP, emphasis added

Living with this incredible demonic activity going on in my life throughout my childhood was the absolute worst. I seldom knew when it was going to occur, and I never really knew what took place when the seizure was active. My family, case workers, and foster families related to me what they witnessed when I was involved in an epileptic seizure. I went through my childhood not ever knowing when this demon would show up and cause people to think that I looked and acted like a monster.

The first time I recall having this demon attack was when I was seven years old. It took place in school on a fall day around Thanksgiving. Our class was preparing to be on television to do a Thanksgiving special. Our teacher was so proud of us, and we too thought we were special. We were expressing joy, laughter, and excitement as we waited. We were busy jostling about, causing a noisy clatter as we tinkered with the special instruments we each would be playing.

I had been assigned a pair of long cymbals that were banged together. If you are not used to the sound they make, it makes your eardrums ring. I stood proudly playing my instrument as directed by my teacher. While I was banging the instrument, the demon spirit began to take over my body. I began to feel jumpy, and the next thing I knew, I was on the floor. I was told that this activity quickly drew a crowd.

My eyes began to roll around, my tongue got thick, and foam came out of my mouth. My body was shaking all over, as if I were on one of those exercise machines. When I regained consciousness, I was lying on my back in a hospital bed with tubes connected to me. I had missed the Thanksgiving special with my class. I had wanted so much to be a part of that special.

It was always so embarrassing at school when these seizures would show up. I was always told by the children or other people what I looked like. With this happening in public, I became a laughingstock, and kids would call me a monster or reject me with a "don't play with her" attitude.

These seizures and the demon of epilepsy controlled my life. They were largely the reason I was sent to so many different foster homes. I took medications for the seizures, and I had a lot of hospital visits. Around that time, a nurse explained to me what they were doing at each of my visits. She explained that the electroencephalogram (EEG) tests were necessary to measure my brain's electrical activity and to detect any abnormalities. An EEG is one of the main diagnostic tests for epilepsy.

I thought the test was kind of weird and something you would see in an outer space movie. I was placed on my back on a bed in a partially dark room and covered with a blanket. Initially, I would feel like I was getting ready to take a nap. The nurse would then attach little needles to wires on my head and one needle in each ear lobe. Probably, about twenty needles in all were used. The needles didn't really hurt. They felt like you had stuck yourself with a pin.

The nurse would then push some buttons on a machine that was nearby and tell me to close my eyes. Sometimes she would tell me to think about different kinds of things, such as what I had done that day or what I had eaten for breakfast. After every EEG test, I had to get my hair washed because they used a sticky substance to attach the needles.

Medical science defines epilepsy as "a neurological disorder marked by sudden recurrent episodes of sensory disturbance, loss of consciousness, or convulsions, associated with abnormal electrical activity in the brain." The word *epilepsy* derives from a Greek word meaning "to hold or seize." Seizures are what happen to people with epilepsy. A seizure has also been characterized as "a fit" or a "spell" (Google web noun: definition and epilepsy; KidsHealth from Nemours).

I had many, many hospital visits and EEG tests. One of the medicines they prescribed to help control my seizures was Dilantin. It and some of the other medications made me sleepy and feel dopey a lot of times. It didn't seem like the drugs were working because even though I was taking them, I continued to have seizures. The drugs couldn't control my seizures, so they certainly never cured me.

One night when Mom was in the hospital, we were staying at Momma Jennie's house, and we had just finished getting ready for bed. Momma Jennie had pulled out her Bible, and we were going to say our prayers before going to sleep. We were lying in bed, and Momma Jennie began talking about Jesus.

Momma Jennie read the story in Luke 9:39 about the boy who had epilepsy. I asked her if Jesus could heal me, because I was tired of all the seizures and everyone making fun of me. She talked to me a little more about the scripture and said, "Yes, Jesus can heal you!"

"Really? Do you think He really can, Momma Jennie?" I asked. "Do you think He can? I am so tired of these seizures and feeling like this."

I was so excited about the Bible story Momma Jennie had read to me and the thought that Jesus could heal me like He had healed the boy in the story that I could hardly sleep that night. All I could think about was getting back to Miracle Temple Church to get prayer.

Finally Sunday came, and I was up first to get ready to go to Sunday school. *How am I going to make it through the whole day until tonight when I can get prayer?* Butterflies were dancing in my stomach. It seemed like the Sunday activities would never end on that day.

At last, we were in the night service. It was 1967, and the Spirit of the Lord was heavy in the service that night. Rev. R. W. Schambach was preaching and teaching about healing. During the altar call, he said, "Anybody need prayer for God to heal them?"

I asked Momma Jennie if I could go up for prayer. She said, "Sure, you can go on up." I jumped out of my seat and made my way to the altar.

Miracle Temple Church was a large building, and there were always lots and lots of people in attendance, especially for the healing services. I was fifteen years old, and I remember standing in line with other people seeking to be healed by God. Reverend Schambach asked me, "What do you want God to do for you?"

I said, "I have epilepsy, grand-mal seizures."

He asked me, "Do you believe that God can heal you of those seizures?"

I said, "Yes! My Momma Jennie read me the story of the boy in the Bible, and I believe!"

Reverend Schambach put his hand on my forehead and began to pray and called that demon of epilepsy out of me. All I remember is that I felt faint. When I came to myself, I was on the floor. I had seen people fall to the floor when getting prayer before, and I knew it was called "being out under the power of God" or "falling out in the Spirit." The ushers helped me up, and I could hear Reverend Schambach saying, "By the power and blood of Jesus, be healed!"

I went back to my seat, smiling and knowing that Jesus had taken the epilepsy away. People said my childlike faith was in operation. I began telling Momma Jennie and everyone seated around us, "I am healed!" I went home and told my mom, Momma Liz, and my siblings that Jesus had healed me. I was healed of epilepsy! I wouldn't let anyone change my mind about what had happened that Sunday night.

I was waiting for the next time that I would go to the doctor for my seizures so I could tell him I was healed. On the next visit to get an EEG, I told the doctor that I had received prayer at church for my epilepsy and believed God had healed me. I did not want to take those EEG tests or the medicine anymore. He looked at me and smiled. I thought he didn't believe me. I thought he was thinking, *This little girl done lost her mind*. But to my surprise, he said, "Well, we will look at your EEG reports from today and go from there."

I was so excited and relieved. I said, "Thank you." I smiled because I didn't mind getting the EEG test on that day, because I knew it would show the results that would prove that God had healed me of epilepsy. I knew *that* EEG test would be my last one.

It seemed like months passed before my next visit with the EEG doctor. The whole time I was waiting to go back for the results of the last EEG test, I did not have any epileptic seizures, since I had received prayer. In the car on the way to see the EEG doctor, I told the case worker all about what had happened to me at church when I got prayer for my seizures. I was sure to tell her that Jesus had healed me, and since He had healed me, I would not be taking the medicine anymore.

The case worker was glad that I hadn't had any more seizures, but she didn't have much to say about my story. She just listened to me talk as she drove us to the appointment. I'm sure she was saying to herself, *This child is making up stories*. But she herself knew that she had not received any reports of seizure activity from my family after that Sunday night prayer. She couldn't explain it, so she decided to just wait and hear the doctor's report.

I could say this was one of the happiest days in my short-lived life. The EEG doctor smiled at me when we walked in. He was holding my file in his hands and told me and the case worker the results of the EEG. The doctor said, "Normal! Your results, Paulette, are normal." He said, "You do not need to take the medication any longer." Then he asked me if I had had any seizures since I had last visited him.

I said, "No, sir," but inside I was shouting, "No, no, no, no! Thank You, Jesus!" The doctor smiled and looked at the case worker, with his eyes gleaming. He asked her for the seizure-activity report on which it was recorded each time I had a seizure. The case worker showed him the report, and the last entry date was a date before the last EEG test. The doctor asked her, "Is this accurate?"

She responded, "Yes, sir, that's accurate. No seizure activity has been reported since that date listed."

When I first arrived in Pittsburgh, Pennsylvania, in 1973, it was necessary to get a physical for my job. Dr. Leslie noticed that I had checked the box on the physical form that read, "Did you have or do you have epilepsy?" I checked the box that indicated "did have." Dr. Leslie questioned me about my history of epilepsy, and I told him that I believed I received a divine healing from God and no longer suffered from seizures. I had been seizure-free for seven years. He asked me to sign a release form so that he could get records from Hahnemann University Hospital in Philadelphia. When he received the seizure records from the hospital and read them, he could not believe it. He realized it was a miracle!

When I share the gospel of Jesus Christ with others, I always tell my testimony about being healed from the nasty demon of epilepsy. I am grateful to God for the ministry of Rev. R. W. Schambach of Miracle Temple Church in Philadelphia. I am not ashamed of healing, not ashamed of the gospel, not ashamed of prayer; and I am thankful to God for what He has done in my life. I am so glad that Rev. R. W. Schambach was obedient to God.

The Word of God reads, "And these signs shall follow them that believe," Mark 16:17a (KJV) I am sixty-three years old, and at the writing of this book, I have not had a seizure, have no symptoms, and have not taken any seizure medications. Do the math: healed for forty-eight years—*seizure-free* !

To God be the glory for the great things He has done!

GROWING UP IN THE KINGDOM OF GOD

---◆-◈-◆---

CHURCH—AFTER MY LIFE WAS CHANGED

My early teenage years were planned by almighty God. Of course, I continued to attend Momma Jennie's church, Miracle Temple, and after accepting Jesus as my Lord and Savior, I became very active in the church. I joined the church and The Ambassadors for Christ choir, a choir of young people, where I found that I too loved to sing. Often I was picked for lead solos. We not only sang at our church, but we were also invited to sing at other churches.

During the summer months, after our own church services, a lot of us teens would go and sing at the A. A. Allen tent services that came to Philadelphia every summer. The minister of music was Gene Martin. He was a phenomenal musician and vocalist. He was in charge of the music at the tent services, and he could bring musical notes out of you that you didn't know you had. He was gifted and anointed in the service of the Lord and was exceptional on the keyboard.

The tent services, or "tent meetings" as they were sometimes called, were always Spirit filled. Singing, preaching, healing, and manifestations of the Spirit of God were always evident during those meetings. Rev. A. A. Allen would preach, and oil would run from his hands. He would stop preaching and call a healing line. Believers would join in the line and extend their faith, and many of them would fall out under the power and presence of God.

Many healings were taking place. People were jumping out of their wheelchairs, throwing down their canes and walkers, and praising God for their healings. Many people would walk away or dance or skip away healed. Others were saying their hearing came back, and others said their vision had been restored. All types of healings were going on. The healing touch from God and the manifested power of God were such powerful things to behold.

In those days, we young people had a solid foundation in the Word of God, and we loved the Lord throughout our Christian journey. We felt it was nothing for us to stay in church all day long on Sunday. We would be there from Sunday school through morning worship; sometimes there would be an afternoon service; and there was always, always a Sunday night service. We had such hunger for God and wanted more and more of His Word.

In Matthew 5:6, the Bible says, "Blessed are they which do hunger and thirst after righteousness, for they shall be filled." We didn't really realize it, but we were getting really filled. We were hungry for the things of God. We loved church and everything that it represented. I thank God for that foundation from years ago. These many years later, all of us (that I know of) have stayed with God and are representing what has been called the fivefold ministry of the Lord, as spoken of in Ephesians 4:11: "And he gave some apostles; and some prophets; and some evangelists; and some pastors and teachers."

Church services were also held on Friday nights, and after the regular service, we would extend the time into an all-night prayer service. We looked forward to this every Friday night. I attended the all-night prayer services from the age of fourteen until I went to college. Every Friday night, I could be found in church. Usually I was somewhere around the altar, seeking God's plan for my life. When I came home on the weekends while in college, I always found my way back to that church altar. I missed church while I was away at college. I visited several churches while away at college, but as the saying goes, "There's no place like home."

All-night prayer services were wonderful. We prayed, sang, and read the Word of God all night long. That is where many of us received the Holy Ghost baptism with the evidence of speaking in tongues. No one went to sleep during all-night prayer, not even the small children. They too were singing, praying, and speaking in tongues. There was no age difference in the Spirit of the Lord. His presence would fill young and old alike. I remember carrying some kids about six or seven years old to their parents' cars on Saturday mornings. Those young kids would be filled with the Spirit and under the power of God. Everyone enjoyed worshiping God and giving Him praise.

I was also part of the witnessing team that went into the community on Saturday mornings. We would pass out tracts and tell whomever we met about Jesus and His love. John 3:16–17 was our motto: "For God so loved the world that he gave his only begotten Son, that whosoever believeth in him should not perish, but have everlasting life. For God sent not his Son into the world to condemn the world, but that the world through him might be saved."

If it was your scheduled time to witness on Saturday, you would have to bring a change of clothes and your toiletries to church with you on Friday so you could change. We knew the importance of being fresh and clean as we witnessed to others about Christ. Even though we had not slept and had been in the presence of the Lord for hours and hours, we were fired up in prayer and ready to minister to people as God gave us the leading.

We had many young people at our church who were full of energy and looking for things to do for the Lord. Dr. Evelyn Graves, an acclaimed playwright, was introduced into our lives. We loved and appreciated her and listened to her every word. We called her "Mother Graves," and she did not have any trouble out of us.

Dr. Graves presented us her plays, and a drama ministry was born in 1968. We young people loved it. Drama was a new way to express our teachings and feelings. In 1971, the Evelyn Graves Drama Productions company was formed. Drama was something new to the body of Christ and had never been presented in churches before that.

Dr. Graves stepped out in faith and, with a determination that she had heard from God, began to present her works in various churches. Many of the older church members didn't understand this new way to present the gospel of Christ, and some were critical of Dr. Graves's calling. Sometimes people referred to the drama ministry as the devil's work. This mainly came from other churches that had not experienced this great work of the Lord. But no matter what was being said about this new work, Dr. Graves held fast. She knew she was working for the Lord. The evidence of her calling was the many souls that came to Christ as a result of these presentations. The Evelyn Graves

Association took on a new name as we grew and grew, and we did many, many drama productions.

I was chosen to be in the first play, which was called *The Rapture*. This was my first acting part. I was cast as the mother of some teenagers who were having a birthday party. The presentation of *The Rapture* had a profound impact on the audience, and many lives were surrendered to the Lord as a result. Dr. Graves had heard God correctly. He was honoring her obedience to Him, and lives were being changed.

Over forty years later, the Evelyn Graves Association has not only blossomed into a drama productions company, but has also birthed a Christian day care, a K-12 Christian school, catering services, a ministry of recovery, a sharing and caring outreach, the Evelyn Graves School of Performing Arts, the Evelyn Graves Bible School, and a church called Evelyn Graves Ministries Church. Dr. Graves has also been instrumental in developing many community-based educational centers in Philadelphia, along with day camps and mentoring for youth. Dr. Graves became a catalyst for improving the quality of life in the urban community through the performing arts.

I am so grateful that she was obedient to what God called her to do. In her obedience, I found a passion for drama and acting. I did not know it at the time, but God dropped a creative drama mantle from this anointed woman of God into my life. This mantle began to grow in my spirit. To date, I have written and produced numerous drama productions that have been performed in churches and seminars in Pittsburgh and Philadelphia, Pennsylvania; Los Angeles, California; and Rochester, New York. My latest production, titled *What to Do in a Dead Situation*, is the modern-day story of Lazarus. Thank you,

Mother Graves, for your rich deposit into my life, which is yet to this day bearing fruit.

Miracle Temple, where we attended church in Philadelphia, used to be a movie theater, but Rev. R. W. Schambach remodeled it into a church. The building was large enough that they built a baptismal pool and placed it on the top part of the altar. The pool had a large mirror attached to it so that everyone sitting in the sanctuary could view, from the comfort of their seats, the ones who were getting baptized.

I was so excited on the day that I was to be baptized. All the candidates for baptism wore long, heavy, white terry-cloth bathrobes over their white clothes. I had put a white swimming cap on my head so that my hair would not get wet. I can still hear Reverend Schambach saying, "You don't need anything on your head; you are getting wet head to toe for Jesus!" So I and the others took off anything that we had on our heads.

I was so looking forward to this outward symbolic display of what had taken place inwardly in my life. Matthew 28:19 states, "Go ye therefore, and teach all nations, baptizing them in the name of the Father, and of the Son, and of the Holy Ghost." Reverend Schambach placed his hands over my arms that were crossed against my chest, and holding my back, he lowered me into the baptismal water very quickly. He was praying in the Spirit, and everyone was singing that traditional baptismal song "Take Me to the Water."

When I came up out of that baptismal water, I felt the power of God all throughout my body. I knew I would never be the same again. Amazingly, my hair didn't get very wet when I was submerged. Only the top of my hair got slightly wet. Throughout my life, whenever I have heard or participated in singing the song "Take Me to the Water," I have relived the memory of that glorious day when I was baptized.

Song service and "shouting" was a Sunday night tradition at our church. The group of young people that I used to associate with loved that service. We had such joy in singing and praising God! "Shouting" was not necessarily a verbal activity; it was generally a physical activity. We watched the older people "shout" and run around the church, thanking God for what He had done in their lives. We youngsters used to talk about what we would look like if we were to "shout."

People who did not understand the traditions of our church were confused when people would get up and "shout" in church, because rarely was the person saying anything. If they were, they were praising God. The "shout" generally consisted of an activity involving their feet and legs. In more recent years, it has been called "dancing before the Lord."

In our group, we made a plan. If any of us were to "shout," someone from our group had to make sure they were watching so they could tell the person how they looked. In one particular Sunday evening service, we were singing praises to the Lord. The presence of the Lord was thick in our midst. I began to feel the presence of the Lord, and I started to jump up and down and sing and verbally shout out the name of Jesus. I wasn't doing any of that to be seen by others. I felt a joy deep inside me that I could not explain, and the only way I could express it was to jump and shout and sing about Jesus. I did not just verbally shout out the name of Jesus, but apparently I engaged in a "shout" dance during that service.

After the service was over, my friends told me the rest of what I had done during that time. They said I was "shouting" with my legs going up and down really fast. I was moving from side to side, while my legs were moving fast. I was moving around so much that I ended up on the other side of the church from where I was sitting. While all of this was going on, sometimes I had my eyes closed, and sometimes they were open. My arms were waving back and forth; one of my shoes came off, and my socks were down to my ankles.

I know I felt really light and free to move while I was "shouting." It felt good. I had had my first "shouting" experience! I laughed when they gave me the description of my "shouting," but when I looked down, I had only one shoe on, and my socks were down to my ankles. I had more "shouting" experiences, and so did the other young people in our group. I too had my chance to tell them how they looked when they were "shouting."

Another highlight in the kingdom of God was testimony service. I enjoyed hearing all about what God had done for some people and what He had promised to do for others. During one such service, an older gentleman, or "Brother," as we called the men, was sitting in a seat close to the front of the church. Our group of young people was sitting in the same section of the church, but farther back and in the middle. Brother stood up after one of the fiery songs we all had just sung. He began to thank God for his life, health, and strength. He went on to say, "I thank God that I am saved right where I stand." Traditionally, a lot of testimonies started out with that statement. Brother continued to talk about various things that God had done for him, and he was very excited about it. He ended his testimony with, "Pray my strength in the Lord," and sat down.

After Brother had been seated for a few moments, I, along with others in our group, noticed that his eyeglasses were slanted and looked like they were sliding off his face. We were smiling and laughing about how odd it looked, and we were wondering why he was not fixing his glasses. We called an usher to go and mention to Brother about his glasses.

The usher approached Brother to help him with his glasses, and she started screaming. Everyone in the service was wondering what was going on. The service came to a halt. We found out that Brother had passed, right there in the service. His last words were giving glory to God for what He had done in his life. Brother had passed from this life to glory right in front of our eyes! Someone called an ambulance, and the authorities came and took Brother out of the sanctuary. You talk about scared—we were! We did not get into trouble for weeks after witnessing Brother's passing.

Second Corinthians 5:1 says, "For we know that if your earthly house, this tent, is destroyed, we have a building from God, a house not made by hands, eternal in the heavens" (NKJV). This scripture came alive to us in the sanctuary that night. Wow!

My beloved Mother: Rosella Hurst
Brown Poindexter

My beloved Grand-Mother: Pauline
Virginia Hurst Brown

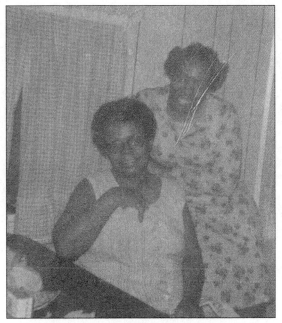

My beloved 2"d Mom: Elizabeth Cobbs Butler
("Momma liz" "Granny") and Me

Me@ the age of 9 (pic. On my soth Cake)

My freshman year @ Northeastern Christian Jr. College (NCC)
Villanova, PA

My Senior High School picture on the button of our
20th year reunion

The "Kool" Gang of NCC, Cheryl, Me, Erik, Mary, Elaine, and AI

Me @ NCC on picture day

The Ambassadors of Miracle Temple Church, Philadelphia, PA

Me one Easter Sunday with some of the youth of Miracle Temple

Me and the Soul Gospel Choir @ NCC, 1969

Me @ NCC my Sophomore year

Me, Sharon Jones, Cheyenne Zellars, NCC roommate's

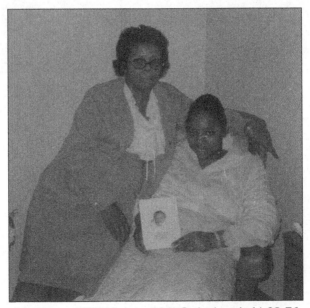

My beloved 2"d Mom and Me@ the hospital4-28-76
(5) days after the birth of our 1st child- Tonita Lynn

Rev. Wiley T. Hill, Asst. Pastor of
Miracle Temple, Philadelphia, PA

Rev. R. W. Schambach, Senior Pastor
of Miracle Temple,
Philadelphia, PA

Dr. Evelyn C. Graves, Founder
of The Evelyn Graves Drama
Productions and Pastor of
Evelyn Graves Ministries,
Yeadon, PA

Me, my loving 2"d Grand-Mom Jennie Ann Cobbs ("Momma Jennie")
2"d Mom - Elizabeth Cobbs Butler 2"d Dad -Joseph Butler ("Daddy Joe")
November 3, 1973

My extended family: My sister Josephine & husband Walt Hudgins
(daughter of Elizabeth & Joseph Butler)

My extended family: My sister Delores "Shorty" Branch and me
(daughter of Elizabeth & Joseph Butler)

My extended family: My sister Paulette Butler Cotton ("Big Paulette") (daughter of Elizabeth & Joseph Butler) along with my nieces Vashti Rose Poindexter Mallard and Larneice Virginia Poindexter (daughters of Joyce Ann Poindexter) along with Rhonda Branch and Michelle Butler-Harding (daughters of Delores Branch)

My extended family: Me and my sister Josephine Butler Hudgins

Mrs. Ruth Staples, Me, Mrs. Hattie Mitchell in Shenandoah, VA

Mrs. Ruth Staples, fancy yellow car in Shenandoah, VA
(we rode around the town in this car)

Mrs. Hattie Mitchell's house in Shenandoah, VA (where I stayed for a week and my Mom would stay here when visiting Ms. Hattie)

Mrs. Ruth Staples and me@ her house in Shenandoah, VA

Mrs. Hattie Mitchell in Shenandoah, VA

Street sign "Shenandoah"

The corner store

The town sign

Me, my baby brother, Michael Anthony Poindexter My older sister
Madelyn "Carol" Brown Britton

Me, my older brother DeWitt Poindexter

Me, my oldest sister Joyce Ann Poindexter
My baby brother Michael Anthony Poindexter

Me, my brother Dewitt Poindexter, sister Joyce Ann Poindexter (when we were
little we always joined hands like this- there were pies but they were lost)

Me, my baby sister Marcia
Poindexter

My High School Photo
(Overbrook- Class of 1969)

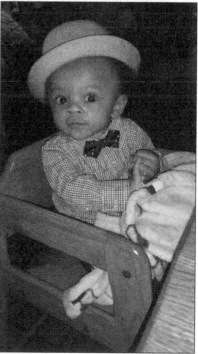

New Grandson: Nathanael
Zamar Davidson

My immediate Family
Son: Minister John T. Davidson, Ill
Daughter: Elder Paulette Elizabeth Davidson
Daughter: Tonita Lynn Davidson
(me)- Rev. Paulette Virginia Brown Poindexter Davidson
Husband: Pastor John T. Davidson, Jr.
Daughter: Mia Ruth Davidson Hines
Grandson: Erik Michael Hines, II
Son: Dr. Erik Michael Hines, Sr.
Grand-daughter: Amara Tomihn Davidson

Graduation from CCAC

(LEFT TO RIGHT): Elaine Cobbs, Cherry Lingbawan, Eddie Poblete, Mr. Brown, sponsor; Abel Udom, Bob Shaw, Joni Newton, Carol Gunselman, Paulette Poindexter.

Me with the Library Staff @ NCC

Me with the Business Club @ NCC

My extended family: My
brother Elbert Butler (son of
Elizabeth & Joseph Butler)

Me singing for the Freshman
Talent Show @ NCC

My Sunday School Teacher- Rev. Dr. Anna Stith-Pugh

Me and others singing during Chapel @ NCC

A Sister Connection – Again

My high school days were lonely and very emotional. I did have some fun and was active with groups and various clubs, but it was emotional because I was just beginning to grow into my teenage years. I was made very aware of the fact that I knew nothing about my biological mom's upbringing or about family members other than Mr. William Brown, my mom's stepdad.

Other students were talking about their moms, and I guess the grieving process was catching up with me. *Who am I? Who is my family? Who are my blood relatives?* All these thoughts and more flooded my mind. I tried to push those thoughts back and forget about them. However, at times, it was very overwhelming.

I had a lot of things on my mind while still in high school. It was getting close to graduation, and I had to finish my coursework, including writing reports, taking final tests, and completing assignments. I was a part of D.E.C.A., which stands for Distributive Education Clubs of America. As part of D.E.C.A., students attended school for half of the day and were part of a work group the other half of the day.

My D.E.C.A. assignment during my senior year was at Schambach Miracle Revival, Inc. I had the opportunity to work with Rev. R. W.

Schambach and other office crew. Edwina, one of my classmates, worked there as well. The office was an exciting place, and we were both excited to work there. My job was to type names and addresses onto metal square plates. The plates were used to address the free monthly magazines issued from the office. We were using an advanced mailing system to reach many, many people, and we knew that our job was very important.

Reverend Schambach would go out "on the field," as he called it, preaching the gospel, praying over people for healing, and witnessing about the power of God. He would close the office on the day of his return and order all types of food and goodies for the staff. During those closed office meetings, Reverend Schambach would relate all the miracles that God had performed while he was out on the field. Reverend Schambach had incredible stories of God's miraculous power and of all the many people he had encountered during his stay on the field. I can still remember him stating his favorite line: "You don't have any trouble; all you need is *faith in God* !"

I was the first one in my immediate family to graduate from high school and go on to college. In 1969, Overbrook High School in Philadelphia promoted more than nine hundred graduates. I was honored to be numbered among them. We held our heads high with dignity and respect as we marched, singing, "Hail to thee, Overbrook High, Your colors we will hold dear. . . ."

In August of 1969, I was accepted into the summer program at Northeastern Christian Junior College located in Villanova, Pennsylvania. Villanova was only about an hour in travel time from Philadelphia, but leaving home was scary and exciting at the same time. Eventually I met new friends and joined an a cappella choir and other clubs. Even though I was very busy with classes and extracurricular activities, I still had nagging thoughts about my family roots and how to satisfy that longing in my soul.

I knew I wanted to find my oldest sister, Carol, again. We had not communicated since that first meeting with Mom when we took the bus ride to Harrisburg as kids. Somehow I remembered Mr. William Brown and his address from that original visit. I could hear "1060 Oberlin Street, Oberlin, Pennsylvania," ringing out in my mind.

Not knowing about my family history and ancestry was beginning to weigh so heavily on me that it became difficult to concentrate on my classes and school assignments. Finally, I admitted to myself, *This is really consuming me. Where is Carol Britton?* I sat down one day and wrote Mr. William Brown a letter. I told him that I was Rosella's daughter and reminded him of our trip to visit him when I was younger. I mentioned that I had seen him at Mom's funeral and hoped that he remembered me. I asked him if he knew my sister Carol's address. I wanted to write to her. I told him a little bit about my attending college and what I was studying and the well-being of my siblings.

Mr. Brown wrote me back, assuring me that he remembered me and restated his love for his stepdaughter, Rosella. Mr. Brown included in his letter the address for my sister Carol. I was so excited that Mr. Brown had given me Carol's address. I looked forward to writing her. I wasted no time in getting a letter off to her. I could not wait to finally connect again with my oldest sister, Carol. But I would have to wait.

College days were filled with studying and going to classes, checking out the different clubs and groups to join, and just being very busy. Even with all that going on, you could still feel lonely for home, family, and friends. No matter how popular you were on campus, no matter how many friends and activities you were a part of, you wanted mail. It was not unusual to see standing room only around the mail room daily. Everyone would pile into the mail room, waiting and hoping for a letter from home or from a friend at another college or another state. Even junk mail would do.

Excitement, smiles, pushing and shoving broke out if you heard your name called for mail. "Paulette Poindexter," as my name was called, "you've got mail!" Ah, those were sweet words to a college student's ears. I would periodically get mail, and that was always very exciting, but I looked for a response letter from my sister Carol. Months went by and nothing—no letter came from Carol. Quite some time later, Carol called me. She never did write. Carol preferred to talk on the phone rather than to write. I learned later from her boyfriend and her daughter Robin that her call to me was with hesitation.

ROBIN TELLS HER STORY

"I grew up believing that my mom, Carol, was an only child. Neither my mom nor my grandparents, Mr. and Mrs. Cornelius Brown, ever spoke of any other children. All that changed on the day that I read a letter that a woman named Paulette had written to my mom. As Mom's boyfriend and I read that letter, my life was changed forever.

"Paulette indicated in her letter that she and my mom were sisters, and even better, they had other sisters and even brothers. At the end of Paulette's letter, she asked Mom to please respond. Mom told us that she had no intention of responding. Mom went on to express other thoughts and feelings about that subject, but we pleaded with her to respond to Paulette—no, my aunt, Aunt Paulette. I had aunts and uncles! I probably had cousins also. We begged Mom to respond.

"Mom's boyfriend pointed out a poignant detail: 'It is not Paulette's fault that she is your sister.' Finally, over the course of several months and repeated inquiries, Mom consented to call Aunt Paulette. When Mom finally talked to Aunt Paulette, I was very happy. We now had knowledge of more family members. How very exciting!

"I was attending middle school at that time, and in response to an assignment from school, I wrote a paper titled 'Two Sisters Meet.' My teacher enjoyed my writing, and I received an A+ as the grade for that paper. That was one of my proudest moments, overshadowed only by the reality that I now had a bigger family. I was so glad that my mom called her sister, my Aunt Paulette. Now a whole new, larger world opened up to us."

In her phone call to me, Carol continued to state that she had always thought of herself as an only child. After all, that is how she was raised in her adopted family. It was difficult for her to consider that someone else was her birth mother and that she had siblings, even though she had met Marcia, Michael, and me several years earlier. She admitted that she had tried to forget about that meeting. Her mom and dad, Cornelius and Anna Brown, rarely spoke of Rosella. Carol admitted that she had thought long and hard about answering my letter, and that her daughter Robin had convinced her to make contact with me.

I asked Carol if she would consider meeting her other siblings: DeWitt, Joyce Ann, Marcia, and Michael. I told her that DeWitt was incarcerated at Camp Hill Prison in Harrisburg and soon due to have a family day. Carol was still living in Harrisburg, so getting to Camp Hill Prison would not be too difficult for her.

Family day at Camp Hill Prison was when an inmate's family would bring food to the prison, join their loved one, and have an outdoor picnic. I told Carol that it would be a great time for her to get to see her siblings. We were all going to attend. DeWitt had sent his food list home, and we were excited about the family day. Carol said she would think about going. We were all hoping that Carol would go and that she would be able to get to know the rest of her blood relatives.

FAMILY DAY AT CAMP HILL PRISON

Carol did come. I was ecstatic when I saw her outside the great wall of the prison. As we approached Carol before we all went through the traditional prison detectors, I reintroduced her to Marcia and Michael. They vaguely remembered each other. I introduced Carol and Joyce for the first time. When we were all cleared and waiting in the family room for them to bring DeWitt down, Carol, Joyce, Marcia, and Michael engaged in small talk. It was so important to me that we siblings bond, because after all, we were family.

Finally DeWitt arrived, and the guards showed us where our picnic spot would be. Tables and benches were set up all over the grounds, and the weather was beautiful. There were so many families out that day, and every table was overflowing with food. Fried chicken seemed to be the meat of the day, along with all the sides, and there were desserts galore.

Everyone was so happy to see DeWitt, and he couldn't get enough hugs from everyone. DeWitt knew that Carol had been invited, and he too had hoped that she would come. He was very glad that she came. Carol was introduced to DeWitt, and in a matter of moments, she went from being an only child to being the oldest of six children. Wow!

DeWitt had several questions for Carol about her life, as we all did. We all had the usual questions of "How many children do you have?" "Are you married?" "Where do you work?" "Tell us about yourself: what are your likes and dislikes?" Of course, we did not have a particular order for our questions, but as we were fellow-shiping and eating, the answers were being provided by Carol. We also filled Carol in on our lives.

One question I asked Carol was, "Why didn't you come to Mom's funeral with Mr. Brown?"

Carol response was, "I didn't know Rosella as my mother, and my mother, Anna, was living. Plus, I felt bad that my own mother had given me up for adoption."

Everyone was surprised how much Carol looked like Mom and Joyce Ann. There was no denying that she was our older sister. We shared a lot of laughter, mingled with a lot of "oh my" moments and solemn faces. Far too soon, our visiting time came to a close. We each promised to keep in touch with the other, and we all promised to write DeWitt and send money to put on his books. It was always sad for me when it was time to go home. I never liked leaving DeWitt at the Camp Hill Prison. I remember the times when I visited him with Mom. I always had that same feeling of sadness when it was time to leave him.

After leaving Camp Hill, everyone tried to keep the promise of keeping in touch as much as they could. It started out well, with everybody writing to each other, and then it began to slow down until there were no more communications at all. I am the writer in the family, so I continued to write to Carol and DeWitt on a regular basis.

Several years after DeWitt was released from Camp Hill Prison, Michael, my younger brother, was sentenced to the very place he had visited with DeWitt and our family at the family day picnic.

Carol would rarely write back, but she would call from time to time. We talked about me visiting her again at her home in Harrisburg. It would be several years later before I actually visited Carol at her home for the second time.

Communication between Carol and me continued through the years, mostly through phone calls. I would write her every so often, but she mainly called. Our relationship evolved to the point of her calling me "Sis." I also established relationships with Carol's children, and we talked periodically.

On September 29, 2011, I went to the mailbox to retrieve our daily residential mail, and it felt like my heart skipped a beat. Amongst my letters and flyers was a wonderful piece of mail. My sister Carol had written me. Carol, who would only ever call me, had finally mailed me a letter. I was delighted.

I quickly opened the envelope, anxious to read its contents, only to discover another surprise. The envelope held a single photo—no letter, nothing in writing, just a photo. I smiled and said to myself, *Yep, that's Carol. She's not a writer.* She still hadn't written, although she did address and mail an envelope to me. The photo was of Carol's adult children: Lionel, Robin, and Susan. I cherished the picture.

I regret that I never took the time to call Carol about the picture. I never spoke with her again. I felt that I would always get around to calling Carol, or she would call me and I'd hear, "Hi, Sis." I was so busy with the responsibilities of family, work, and church that I didn't get to call and tease her about actually sending me mail.

On October 28, 2011, about a month later, I was on a long-distance phone call with Carol's son, Lionel. Lionel and his family were living in North Carolina. Our call was interrupted. Lionel was informed that his mother, Carol, had suffered a massive heart attack while at a gas station in Harrisburg and had been rushed to the hospital. Lionel was just about to hang up from our call and reach out to his sisters, when our call was interrupted again. Lionel was informed that his mother, Carol, had been pronounced dead at the hospital. Lionel, Robin, and Susan's mother—my oldest sister, Carol—was gone forever.

I REMEMBER MOM—ROSELLA HURST BROWN POINDEXTER

Music and singing were a constant in our young lives and has continued into my adult life. Many times as children, we would wake up to the sound of Mom softly singing around the house. That was one of the comforting ways to wake up and realize that I was home with Mom. Rarely did foster parents sing; besides, Mom had a beautiful voice.

Mom had two special songs that she enjoyed and would sing all the time. It was always exciting to hear Mom sound out a rousing rendition of "Life Is a Ball Game" by Wynona Carr. Mom would often sing this song in the afternoons, enjoying belting out the verses that talked about Bible heroes and their positions in the ball game called "life." While Mom was cooking, cleaning, or doing other things around the house, she would sing "Ball Game," as well as another of her favorites. Mom also loved the song "The Old Rugged Cross," the old hymn written by Rev. George Bennard.

THE OLD RUGGED CROSS

On a hill far away stood an old rugged cross,

The emblem of suffering and shame:

And I love that old cross where the dearest and best

For a world of lost sinners was slain.

So I'll cherish the old rugged cross,

Till my trophies at last I lay down;

I will cling to the old rugged cross,

And exchange it some day for a crown.

George Bennard

Mom's beautiful voice soothed some of the sadness I had experienced from being shifted through multiple foster placements. I didn't know it at the time, but I learned that I too love to sing, and several of my family members have also inherited the gift of singing. When I was younger, I wondered where that gift came from. My older sister Carol helped me with that piece of our history.

Carol related the story of someone who lived in Harrisburg who had known our grandmother, Pauline. It had been reported that our grandmother, Pauline Hurst Brown, was an excellent singer. She could be heard singing from blocks away. Grandma Pauline's voice was beautiful, and it soothed anyone in earshot. As Grandma Pauline had a big, booming voice, people would slow down as they passed her area, just to hear her beautiful melodies. No doubt, Mom had often heard her mother singing throughout the day and through any given situation.

Grandma Pauline had other wonderful qualities and attributes. Folks would tell stories that Grandma Pauline could sew anything.

If she saw you with a dress on during the day, she would have that same dress made by evening, using no pattern. Wow, what creativity, and it still runs through our family's generations. You can't run or hide from your DNA—it catches up with you.

I actually lived with my mom for only a brief period after getting out of the foster homes. But those short-lived years were very special. Mom was a nurse's aide at a hospital, but she had to stop working when her health began to fail. I didn't know all of Mom's medical concerns, but I knew the doctors had told her to stop smoking and drinking. Every time I could, I would jokingly slide in the question and its answer: "Mom, are you supposed to be smoking?" I would ask. "Noooo!" I would then answer for her. Mom would give me that look only she could give. We all knew what that look meant: if we knew what was good for us, we would be quiet and mind our own business. We knew that look well, and oh yes, we respected it.

Mom was creative when it came to her cigarettes. Mom would send us children outside to pick up cigarette butts from the ground. We hated doing this. People would watch us picking up the butts as they passed. They would suck their teeth and mumble about us being bad kids. We all had to take turns at scrounging for butts off the street. I don't know about Michael and Marcia, but I think I hated it the most. My brother and sister probably hated it as much as I did, because we used to fight over whose turn it was to go out and scavenge.

The corner store sold cigarettes in increments of three for a quarter. Did Mom not have a quarter, or did she just enjoy rolling her own cigarettes? She would take the butts, remove all the tobacco from them and use those small thin sheets of paper to roll her own cigarettes. Sometimes Mom's tab at the local store would be maxed out, or maybe she just didn't want to give up her change. "I can roll my own," she would say. She was happy to do just that.

When Mom received her welfare check, she always bought one of us a new outfit, but she said we had to take turns. If this month was my month, Marcia and Michael would have to wait. When it was not your turn, of course you would always try to beg for something, trying to pull on Mom's heartstrings. I can hear her firmly stating, "It's not your month!" Mom would chuckle, knowing that we were joking. We each knew the rules.

When it was your month, excitement was in the air and expectation was close by. Even if you only got a pair of $2.99 sneakers or a top or a shirt or whatever, you were excited because you were receiving something new. We could have whatever we wanted for our month. At least it seemed that way to us kids. I'm sure Mom helped to guide us in the direction best suited to her budget. Whatever that special something was, it was always over and above the regular necessities that Mom would buy from time to time.

Mom was an avid bingo player. Bingo was held every Friday at Saint Theresa's Catholic School on Broad and Catherine Street in Philadelphia. Mom would use half of one of those long banquet tables and fill it with lots and lots of bingo cards. We never knew how many cards Mom used when she played, but it seemed like a hundred or more.

Mom had all the necessary equipment to play, which included her trinkets, or charms. Mom carried all her stuff for the game in her bingo bag. When Mom got to bingo, she would carefully set out her chips, ink markers, tape, trinkets, etc. The tape was vital to keep the large number of cards in order during the game. We all thought those trinkets or knickknacks were a strange part of the bingo game, but Mom was not alone in her actions. Many of the bingo players were very, very serious about their game and all the parts necessary for them to win. Mom was very good at the game, and she yelled bingo a lot.

Marcia and I would often go with her. We liked going to bingo on Friday nights. We would be sure to wear our sneakers, because although we were too young to play the game of bingo, we were able to make some serious side money. At least it was serious money to us. It was more than we had entered Saint Theresa's with. Our pockets would be heavy and jingling from all our coins. We earned our money by being the "legs" for the bingo players.

Saint Theresa's hall was crowded from the front of the room to the back with people trying their luck at bingo. Sometimes, if the jackpot was big enough, the room would have almost 150 people in it. Those serious players rarely left their cards, but we could spot a person who was just about ready to munch on something. All the kids in attendance would rush around, asking the players if they wanted something to eat. Concentrating on the numbers being called out for bingo was a full-time job for the players, but their stomachs would growl for snacks. That's where we came in.

We kids kept the players supplied with soda, coffee, chips, cookies, sandwiches, and whatever was on sale that night. The grateful players would tip us for our help. We soon learned who liked relish on his hot dog and who wanted crackers rather than chips. Sometimes the players who knew us would just say, "Bring me something, quickly." We made quite a bit of change that way. At times, we would give Mom some of our stash to buy more bingo cards.

But the highlight of the evening was to rip the taped bingo cards off the tables when it was over. We were always surprised and happy about the number of coins found under the bingo cards. The players didn't care; they just walked away, either very happy at having won or disappointed at having lost. Either way, they would be back the next Friday.

Mom was fascinated with numbers. She loved "playing numbers" and would hit often. Mom would get her numbers from just about anywhere. I remember her getting numbers off the silver lining in the Pall Mall cigarette pack once. How in the world did Mom ever find out that numbers were in the lining of the pack? I looked for myself one day, and yes, there were numbers printed there. Mom would somehow put them together and hit. She would be excited and say, "I hit!"

Mom had been directed to stop drinking by the doctor, but she said she was grown and could do whatever she wanted to do. Her favorite drink was sloe gin. It was a dark-red drink, but Mom would put milk in it, and then it looked like a strawberry milkshake. But it was nothing like a milkshake when I took a sip once. As a child, I was not sure why they called it sloe gin. Maybe it was because when she drank it, she would slowly become tipsy. In a slow kind of fashion, Mom would shift from being fine to becoming a little woozy, then being tipsy, after sipping on a sloe gin for a while.

Mom would begin to act slightly strange once she became tipsy from her sloe gin. Marcia and I caught on to Mom's odd behavior after watching her sip her sloe gin, so we would go to bed and act like we were asleep. Mom would start calling us, but we would not answer. We would lie very still when she would come into the room. We would hear her ask, "Y'all asleep already?" Then she would go out of the room, believing us even though she heard our fake snores.

Did Mom know that we were faking? Probably so, because moms always know that kind of stuff.

One night Mom was a little tipsy. After she had called us and we had faked through her call, she went to the kitchen and started frying chicken. Who can resist the smell of chicken frying? We knew Mom was frying that chicken in hot grease in a big cast iron skillet, and we knew it wasn't just going to be chicken. Mom always had yummy sides with her hot fried chicken, and sometimes cornbread. Our mouths began watering. Chicken wings were our favorite.

We couldn't resist any longer. Fake sleep went out the window. We jumped out of bed, ran to the chicken, and pulled chairs up to the table, asking for hot fried chicken and sides. Mom laughed and said, "Uh-huh, I thought you girls were asleep." We were busted about the fake-sleep thing, but we figured Mom knew we weren't asleep anyway. But busted or not, we were sitting down to eat hot, juicy fried chicken, and it was so, so good!

When Mom was tipsy, she used to talk about things from her past. At the time that it was occurring, though, I did not realize they were memories. Mom would call out the names of people that we had never heard of before. She would just be talking to them and giving them a piece of her mind. Mom wouldn't hold back on what she was saying to them. Then, just as quickly, she would pop back and start talking about things that were going on right then.

One night I had not yet escaped to bed to fake sleep when Mom saw me in the hallway upstairs. Mom grabbed me on the left side of my neck. Her very long fingernails gripped my neck and dug into my skin. Mom began calling me by somebody else's name and shook me. Mom actually thought that I was this other person that she was yelling at. From what I could tell from the conversation, this person

Mom had called me had done something to her, and she was really telling this person off. But all the while, Mom's natural nails were digging deeper into my neck.

I began to yell out, "Mom, stop! It's Paulette." I had to keep on saying it. Finally I was screaming out, "Mom, stop! It's me, Paulette. Mom, you're hurting me!"

Mr. Shots came running to my rescue. "Shots," as Mom called him, was her boyfriend. Mr. Shots was downstairs in the kitchen arranging sandwiches in the refrigerator. He was a kind man who had a medium build and wore a hat all the time. Mr. Shots was a hard-working man. He worked at a cafeteria near Broad Street in Philadelphia. The cafeteria would often have food left over that was too good to throw out. Mr. Shots would always bring tons of sandwiches and desserts of all varieties to our house.

He was the only boyfriend that my mom ever had that we loved. Yes, we loved the sandwiches and desserts and goodies, but it was more than that. Mr. Shots would play games with us. One game I remember was when he would do the "take his finger off" trick. But we loved Mr. Shots because he loved Mom and us unconditionally, and it showed. Mom at times would treat him badly, but he kept coming around, and deep down I believe they loved each other.

Mr. Shots heard me yelling, and he ran upstairs and into the hallway. "Zeke!" he yelled. "Zeke, what are you doing to the girl?" Mom was just rambling on and on to the person that she thought she held captive. "Zeke, let her go!" he yelled. I guess Mr. Shots's yelling out to Mom broke her out of that trance or whatever she was experiencing. She let me go.

Crying, I ran to the bathroom to look at my neck, while Mr. Shots tried to calm Mom down. The side of my neck was bleeding. I took a wet washcloth and started dabbing my neck. The bleeding stopped after a while, but my neck was hurting quite a bit. I went to bed, confused about what all had just happened.

The next day, I got up for school as usual, and when I looked into the mirror, of course it had not been a bad dream. The marks were still there on my neck. The mark seemed to have the shape of a plus and a minus sign. I found some Band-Aids to put on my neck so no one could see the mark at school. Mom was downstairs in the kitchen fixing breakfast for us. I told her I was leaving for school, when she noticed the Band-Aids on my neck. She asked, "What happened to your neck?"

I looked at her in disbelief. Thoughts began swirling in my head: *Does she really not know what happened last night? How could she forget that she was choking me and that her fingernails were digging into my neck? Doesn't she remember that Mr. Shots shook her to bring her back to herself so that she would let me go? Does she really not remember?*

I couldn't figure it all out, so I made up a story. I said, "I burned myself with the hot curlers when I was curling my hair." That was the only thing I could think of really fast.

Mom said, "Didn't I tell you about playing in your hair with those hot curlers?" All the while, Mom was approaching me and snatched the Band-Aids off my neck. "You won't listen," Mom said, "then don't be trying to hide it."

I left to go to school, knowing kids were going to ask me about what had happened. I was really puzzled. Mom really did not remember what she had done to me. I was a timid child, and I wasn't going to tell her what had really happened. I don't know if Mr. Shots ever told her or not. Thankfully, I never saw that side of Mom again.

Church folks would say that a demon spirit had jumped on her that night. Whatever it was, it scared me, and the scar stayed on my neck for a very long time.

During the brief time we were with Mom, as a family we had many ups and downs, joys and sorrows. We moved a lot, but all of that was okay because we were together and we were family, not pretend as in the foster placements. We played games together. Mom taught us how to play the card game 500. Our winnings were only water, if you lost and your cards in your hand totaled five or more you had to drink those many glasses of water, but we enjoyed that game.

Not too long after the "plus and minus" mark on my neck that Mom thought was from me using the hot curlers, she began to notice that I was doing a pretty good job with hair. She began to allow me to do her hair. I would fancy her hair in different kinds of styles, and she liked them well enough to wear them outside. I began to get so good at it that I thought I was going to be a beautician. I was doing everyone's hair, and they appreciated it because I did a good job.

Mom sacrificed and did without of a lot of things so that we could have what we needed. Mom wasn't strict, but she was firm. We knew right from wrong. We knew what we were allowed to do and what would get us into trouble with Mom. But don't let one of the neighbors say something negative about us! Mom would go off on them verbally, but when she was finished, they thought and felt like blows had been exchanged.

My mom's heart was toward us kids even though she was full of hurts and had open wounds in her heart. In one of our many heart-to-heart conversations, I remember Mom telling me the story of how we first got placed into foster care. She wanted us to be with her so many times, but it was a long time coming. I could feel Mom weeping through her words, and the "I am sorry" was definitely soaked into her story.

Mom did the absolute best that she could within her circumstances and through all the areas in which she was tormented. Mom loved us and wanted to do right by her children, but she needed help from her many, many hurts. As a child, I didn't understand fully all that was going on in my childhood. I didn't fully understand Mom's pain and her decisions. I didn't fully understand why our lives had unfolded the way that they had, based on Mom's choices. I didn't realize that Mom was hurting and needed help herself. I didn't know how to help Mom. I didn't even know that she needed help. I didn't understand adult things at that age, but I knew that Mom loved us.

I thought Mom was beautiful, and I loved her very much. Later in my life, I learned that God too saw Mom as beautiful. Candice Glover, a young singer and songwriter, wrote a song titled "Beautiful." When I hear the words of her song, I think of my beautiful mother and the scripture in Psalm 139:14 that declares, "I am fearfully and wonderfully made."

When I was close to being fourteen, Mom got very sick and was diagnosed with malignant hypertension, which was causing her kidneys to fail. As a result of this illness, Mom experienced multiple stays in the hospital and never got back to Carol's or Mr. Brown's home ever again.

While Mom was in and out of the hospital, Momma Liz, Mom's sister-friend, took care of us. Each time Mom was released from the hospital, Momma Liz always cared for her also. As the oldest daughter involved with our mom at that time, I felt that she knew she was very sick. Mom had needed for us to meet our oldest sister, Carol, and our step-grandfather, Mr. Brown. That trip to Harrisburg had a profound purpose. I was too young for my mother to disclose all the information to me, but Mom knew I would figure it out. She knew her child.

As Mom's health continued to fail, she depended on Granny to take care of us. Mom was in and out of the hospital frequently. In May of 1967, I spent my fifteenth birthday in the hospital at Mom's bedside. Mom was experiencing a rough time medically, and I was reading to her from my Bible.

I was a young Christian and didn't have a lot of experience with Christianity, and neither did I have deep spiritual knowledge. I did not know many of the proper and encouraging words or prayers or promises of God to say to my mom. I was just learning about Jesus, and I didn't yet know how to tell Mom about Him. She seemed so weak and didn't say much.

I would visit Mom as often as I could while she was in the hospital. I didn't even know all the reasons Mom was in and out of the hospital, but I knew they were trying to help her. I didn't have all the words to say, so I just stayed close to her bedside, touching her arms and hands to let her know I was with her. I was just glad she was in the hospital and getting the help she needed. When Mom was at home suffering, Granny would say, "I am taking you to the hospital." Mom would put up a fuss at times and would not want to go.

The preacher at church often talked about people going to heaven. He would say, "You must be saved to inherit eternal life." At that time, I wasn't sure what all that meant, but I wanted Mom to go to heaven if she died. I prayed really hard that she would be saved.

"Hello," Granny said into the telephone. "Yes, this is she." I watched as Granny's face broke down into sadness. Granny said,

"All right, thank you," as she hung up the phone. Tears began to slide down Granny's cheeks.

"What is it, Granny? What happened?" I asked.

Granny said, "Go get Marcia and Michael." We three returned to Granny, and after instructing us to sit down, Granny told us that there would be no need to go back to the hospital anymore.

"Why, Granny, why?" we chorused.

Granny continued by saying, "Well, children, your mom has passed on into heaven. Her suffering is over. She is with Jesus."

It was Saturday morning, August 12, 1967. I could hear the adults whispering downstairs, but I could not hear them clearly. I knew they were discussing Mom and what they needed to do next. I remember crying when Granny first told us about Mom's death, and then all sorts of things flashed through my mind. I wondered, *Did Mom get saved? What happened to her? Why can't we see her? What now? What about us?* My heart was racing. Mom! Mom! My mom had died. I wanted to call my friends from church. They were my life, and we always talked about everything. I needed to be with and talk to my friends right then.

I was overwhelmed by grief and sadness at the death of my mom, and the only way I knew to deal with it at that time was to write. I sat down to express the thoughts in my head and created the poem "She Overslept."

She Overslept

It is Monday morning—time
For my mom to get my breakfast fixed.

She overslept.

It is Monday afternoon—time
For my mom to get my lunch fixed.

She overslept.

It is Monday evening—time
For my mom to get my dinner fixed.

She overslept.

Alone—withdrawn—confused
People ask, "Where is your mom?"

She overslept.

Some whispered, "Death." My heart aches.
To the outside world she died. To me

She overslept.

(This poem was published in the *Different Drummer* publication of the Community College of Allegheny County, Pennsylvania, South Campus, 1989. Out of 2,500 entries in the Community College magazine category, this publication was awarded first place!)

Granny called Mr. William Brown in Oberlin, Pennsylvania, and said to him, "Mr. Brown, this is Elizabeth Cobbs Butler. You remember, Rosella's friend in Philadelphia. Well, Mr. Brown, Rosella's battle is over. She has passed on into heaven."

Granny and Mr. Brown discussed Mom's illnesses and the last few years of her life and her passing while in the hospital. Mr. Brown persuaded Granny to hold all the services on the same day, because he did not drive well at night and did not want to have to go back and forth from Oberlin to Philadelphia.

In Philadelphia, traditional funeral arrangements were to have an evening viewing for a few hours before the eulogy. The casket would remain open during the eulogy, and a thin white hankie would be placed over the deceased's face during the services. After the services, everyone would go up again to view the body before going home. The next morning, everyone would return to the church for another viewing, and then finally the casket would be closed. Then it was time to go to the cemetery for burial. Family and friends would gather together afterwards to eat and share their stories about their loved ones.

It seemed like months before Mom's funeral was actually held, but it was only maybe a week. I didn't understand why it took so long to have her funeral, for us to say our final good-byes and go to the cemetery. Granny took us to get new outfits for Mom's funeral. Shopping used to be fun. This trip was not fun. The clothes were nice, but we were buying outfits to say good-bye to our mother. I wore a light-blue striped seersucker suit. I was too nervous and anxious to do my own hair, so I got my hair done at the nearby beauty salon.

The day of the funeral was so strange—strange because I had been back with my real mom for such a short time and then she was taken away from me again. It felt strange because I didn't think we should have been burying our mother at her age. It felt strange because TV and the movies depicted mothers living to a ripe old age and being there to help daughters understand boys. It felt strange because mothers helped daughters pick prom and wedding dresses. It felt strange because mothers helped new moms understand the birth of their first child. It felt strange because moms loved and doted on their grandchildren. It felt strange because of all of the times I had been taken away from my mom and placed in foster homes, this was the first time that Mom was taken away from me.

I sat there crying and crying. *How could this have happened? Mom was only forty-two years old. I am only fifteen years old. I need my mom!* I screamed internally. I was getting mad at God. He could have changed everything. He could have let me keep my mom until I grew up. *Why did Mom have to die?* I breathed heavily, and my heart ached.

People were passing by Mom's casket for the viewing and saying, "I am sorry," or "You have my sympathy." The looks on their faces showed they were sorry for us. I thought they felt sorry for us because they were thinking, *Now these young kids have no mother.* My friends from church came, and they shared their sorrow with me. It felt good to have friends around me at that time.

I was trying to stop crying to see what was going on in the service. I had asked Granny if someone could sing Mom's favorite song, "The Old Rugged Cross." Mom used to sing that song almost daily, and I knew she would have wanted it sung. While Mom's favorite song was being sung, I started wondering if she had asked Jesus into her heart and if she was going to heaven like Granny had said. I just felt so bad and started to cry all over again, just thinking about it.

It was time in the service for family and friends or whomever to come up and speak about Mom. I knew some of the people who came up to speak, but I didn't know all of them. Some of them I had seen before, but I didn't really know them. A white man stood up to say something. The room got really quiet. I said in my mind, *We don't know any white people in our neighborhood. At least I don't know any that knew Mom.* Everybody was listening to hear what this unknown man had to say about Mom.

Who can this be? I wondered. *Did Mom know him from her childhood? Did Mom work for him somewhere? Is he one of the doctors? Why would one of Mom's doctors come to her funeral?* I watched as he made his way up to the front to speak. He was a very tall gentleman with a slender build. He did not look old, but he wasn't too young either.

He told us his name and offered condolences to our family. As he spoke, he told us that he was a missionary. As such, he made hospital rounds to visit patients, and my mom was on his visitation list. He said that he would read scriptures to Mom and that they would have prayer each time that he visited. He mentioned that he had gone out of town on business, and when he returned to the hospital to visit my mom, the nursing staff told him that she had passed on. He said he had to find out where her services were to be held.

The tall gentlemen went on to say that his interest was not just to say good-bye to our mom, but to let her family and friends know that she had accepted Jesus as her Lord and Savior during one of his visits. "Now Rosella is with the Lord," he said.

I sat there in amazement. Wow! God is concerned about us, and He does answer our prayers. Mom was with the Lord. Those were beautiful words to my ears and heart. I think I stopped crying for a little while, but still I was sad, knowing Mom would never be back. I did not get an opportunity to speak to the missionary before he left. I don't remember him staying very long. But I was grateful to

God that he took the time to come by and give me peace concerning Mom's salvation.

Time moved on, and it seemed like we were just getting back to normal. We continued doing kid things in the neighborhood. I remember going outside and playing jacks and other games with my friends. We played double Dutch, Chinese jump rope, pick-up sticks, and other street games. After dark, we would play Hot-Cold Butter Beans, Come and Get Your Supper, hide-and-seek, and other games. Sometimes we made up games as we went along. It was fun to rip and run up and down the street in front of the houses, playing with friends while family watched over us.

No one talked to us much about our feelings. I guess since we were playing, that could have been a sign that we were okay. I was *not* okay! I thought about Mom a lot and the things we had done together. The funeral kept playing in my mind, and I often had dreams.

Granny told us that Mrs. Watson from the Women's Christian Alliance was coming to talk to us. Marcia and Michael looked at me and asked, "What does she want? Will she try to make us move? Now that Mom is gone, will we have to go too?" When Mrs. Watson came, she told us that she had sad news for us. She told us that we probably would have to go back into the system because Granny and Daddy Joe, her husband, had separated. She said we couldn't stay with Granny because foster care regulations stated that there must be both a mom and dad in the same household. She stated that Granny had just been helping my mom out since she was sick. Now that Mom had passed, it would be necessary for us to return to foster placement.

I stood up and screamed, "I am not going back. I will run away if I have to go back!" By that time, I had taken all that I could take. I became very angry. I had already suffered under the hands of foster parents and their relatives in all kinds of ways, and I was not going to go back. "I love it here with Momma Jennie, Granny, and Daddy Joe. I will not go back. I will not go back," I repeated. "Daddy Joe is here all the time, and he comes and takes us places."

Tears were streaming down my face, and everyone knew that I was serious about not going back. I was the quiet, compliant one. I was the one who always did as I was told—but not now, not anymore! My mom was dead, foster people had mistreated me all of my life, and my dad was dead. All I had left were my sisters and brothers, Momma Jennie, Granny, and Daddy Joe. It didn't matter that two of my sisters were in different cities or that one of my brothers was incarcerated. No matter where they were, they were still family, just like Momma Jennie, Granny, and Daddy Joe. I wasn't going anywhere!

Looking at me, Mrs. Watson said, "I see!" Addressing Granny, Mrs. Watson said, "Well, I will need to talk things over with the staff at the agency, but I will get back to you as soon as I can. In the meantime, the children can remain here with you."

Granny assured Mrs. Watson that she and Daddy Joe were still married and that he did come around a lot and could come around even more. Granny did not want to give us up. It would be only Marcia, Michael, and me under Granny's care, since Joyce and DeWitt were over eighteen years old. Joyce had been living on her own for years, and DeWitt was still incarcerated.

After Mrs. Watson's news of us having to return to foster care, I began to have flashbacks of all the abuse and drama I had gone through in those placements. I still had never told anyone about the horrible things that had happened to me. I couldn't understand why things happened like they did in foster care. I hadn't asked to be a foster child, but in the foster homes, they treated you like it was your fault or like it was something you did to end up in the system.

It was even worse when you stayed in a home that had biological children. Those foster families always treated their own children superior to the "system kids." Maybe those parents had a right to prefer their own children over the kids supplied by the foster care system, but did they have the right to make a foster child feel worthless or unwanted? Where was the love for a child? Some say it was all about the money. Could the system have been paying that much money for a child? It was almost like the history of selling slaves. Slaves were purchased and then abused. Foster children were paid for on a monthly basis and then abused. I just didn't understand it all.

I began to think of ways to run away and where I would go if Mrs. Watson came back and said we could not stay with Granny. *This cannot happen again,* I thought. *I must stay with Granny. I just lost Mom; I can't lose Granny too.*

That night as I lay in the bed, I was rocking back and forth. That was the way that I tried to find comfort. Whenever I was troubled or scared and trying to get to sleep, I would rock back and forth. I had a dream or maybe a vision, but it was real to me.

I was sitting in the Chew Funeral Home on Christian Street in Philadelphia, where my mother had been laid out. I was in the parlor by myself, and Mom's casket was up in front. I could see Mom in the casket from where I was sitting. I was crying and crying, with my head down. I heard some noise coming from up front where Mom was in the casket. I lifted my head and looked at the casket and was shocked by what I saw. I could not move. My eyes opened so wide. I could not believe what I was seeing. Mom was rising up out of the casket and was coming towards me. I began to say, "Mom is coming back! Mom is coming back!"

I must have been getting really loud during that dream because Granny was shaking me awake and saying, "What were you dreaming?" I told her what I had seen in the dream, and she said, "No more funerals for you; you're not even coming to my funeral." We laughed and hugged, and she told me everything was going to be good. Granny stayed with me until I fell back asleep.

Granny knew what she was talking about—good it was! Mrs. Watson came to visit us a few days later with her report on where we were going to be living. She came in smiling, so I was hoping it was good news. It was! We were going to be living with Granny; she was going to be our new mom! She was a foster parent on paper, but in her heart, she was our mom, and she never called us foster children. We were her children. Granny was very loving and had our best interests at heart. Besides, we had known Granny all our lives.

We were going to be a large family now. Granny already had four grown children who lived on their own: Josephine; Delores, whom everybody called Shorty; Elbert; and Big Paulette. My sister Joyce's daughter lived with us; her name was Vashti Rose, and she was two years old. Then there were Marcia, Michael, and I. Joyce and DeWitt were grown and not living with us, but they would always be a part of our family.

God's plan for my life was still unfolding!

Mom would be ninety years old if she were still living today. Before her death, she got to see only four of her grandchildren. Mom was an only child, but she birthed six children. Oh, if she could just see her legacy now! One daughter, Carol, and one grandson, Jahmel, have gone on to be with her. But Mom's legacy continues.

To date, the descendants of Rosella Hurst Brown Poindexter number twenty-two grandchildren, thirty-one great-grandchildren, sixteen great-great-grandchildren, and many more to come.

As an adult and while living in Pittsburgh, I talked with a woman who is gifted to interpret dreams with Christian clarity. I shared my childhood dream with her concerning my mom coming out of her casket. The woman helped me understand that although my mom was indeed deceased, her getting up and stepping out of the casket was representative of the resurrection power of her spirit with God. The woman's scriptural reference was 2 Corinthians 5:8: "We are of good courage, I say, and prefer rather to be absent from the body and to be at home with the Lord" (NASB). The woman went on to say that God, through the dream, was confirming to my heart what I already knew, hoped, and desired, and that was that my mother was at peace in the presence of the Lord. I would get to see her again!

Rosella Hurst Brown Poindexter—I remember Mom with love!

ELIZABETH COBBS BUTLER

lizabeth Butler was affectionately known as "Momma Liz" to her friends and as "Granny" to all the children who loved her. Granny was a hard-working woman. She would always get up early—I mean, really early. Granny would cook us breakfast before we went to school. You were not getting out of the house without cream of wheat, oatmeal, or Ralston to eat. Granny had to get dressed and go to work as well. On Saturdays, we would get the big breakfast spread. Granny would serve pancakes, eggs, grits, bacon, and scrapple. If we had chitlins for dinner the night before, we had them the next morning fried with eggs for breakfast. Fried chitlins tasted like crispy bacon.

Granny taught me how to cook, mostly by my watching her or just by helping with the preparation. When it came to cleaning and cooking chitlins, that was off limits for everyone but Granny. She would stand at the sink for hours, pulling on and stretching those chitlins. All the while, she would be mumbling, "Nobody can clean these but me. I know how to get them good and clean." I used to stand beside her and watch her clean them and wonder if there would be any meat left after she had pulled off so much skin and fat.

Granny had a special ingredient she added to the pot so that you could never tell she was cooking chitlins. Folks used to say chitlins had an awful smell to them when you were cleaning or cooking them. Not Granny's. You would not know that Granny was cooking chitlins unless you saw her cleaning them. Chitlins was one dish that I did not ever cook. I never really learned how to clean them, and then I lost interest in them later in life.

Granny worked at a factory that made blouses for Catholic students. The blouses were part of their uniform. Sometimes Granny would have to work on Saturdays. Part of her job was to clip threads from the blouses and then steam and press them. Before going to work, Granny would cook a meat for dinner and tell me to fix sides later for the meal.

You could hear Granny downstairs doing her hair. Granny would wash her hair, towel it dry, and run a hot straightening comb through it. You would be lying in bed and could smell Granny "frying her hair," as we called it. She would not burn herself. We knew what she was doing because we could smell the hair sizzling, but also Granny had done our hair like that plenty of times. With a towel over her arm, a straightening comb in her hand, and Royal Crown grease on the back of her other hand, Granny's hair would sizzle all the way to dry, pressed, and curled, and she would look good.

One of Granny's best friends was a woman named Ms. Piggy. Those two relied on each other for everything. They talked about everything and laughed and cried together. We enjoyed going down to Ms. Piggy's house. She would cook some delicious dishes. She was raising her grandson, and we had lots of fun playing outside when the weather was nice. I remember playing outside one day and I got thirsty, so I ran into the house to get water. There was a glass on the table with water in it. I grabbed the glass and was about to drink it all; I was so thirsty.

Granny screamed out, "That's not water!" Just as I lifted the glass to my mouth, I stopped short. Granny was right. It did not smell like water. It was straight gin mixed with a little water. We all laughed about it. Granny loved her gin. I think that was not only Granny's favorite drink, but it may have been her only drink.

We all got a wonderful surprise one day. Two years after Mom had passed, Granny answered the telephone one day. "Hello. Yes, this is she. Oh my God! Okay, I'll be right there as soon as I can." Granny hung up the phone. Granny grabbed the sides of her face and said, "Oh my Lord, we've got another one!" Granny picked up the phone and called her friend Ms. Piggy. Shortly thereafter, Granny left home, saying she had to go shopping. Granny and Ms. Piggy met and picked up a few items.

When Granny and Ms. Piggy returned, Granny rang the door-bell, her arms full. When I opened the door and saw Granny holding a baby all wrapped up in new blankets, my mouth dropped open wide. I couldn't believe what I was seeing. Where did Granny get a brand-new baby? Ms. Piggy came in behind Granny, smiling and carrying bags of new-baby stuff. Ms. Piggy had given Granny money to help get the necessary things to bring the baby home.

Later Granny explained that the call had come from the hospital. Apparently, Joyce had given birth to another baby and had named her daughter Larniece Virginia. Joyce had given the authorities Granny's name and number since she could not keep Larniece. Here I was an aunt again at my young age, and now Vashti Rose had a new sister. I smiled as if to say, "Welcome, Larniece. Come on and join the family."

Granny was getting up in age, and some folks said, "Why is she taking on more children—and a baby at that?" Granny did not care what family or friends might say or think. Her heart was just that big. Larniece was just another part of our family.

Granny was always an encouragement in my life. She would praise and congratulate me for all my accomplishments, whether at school, a new job, college, marriage, or the birth of my children. Granny lived to see two of my four children. When I gave birth to Tonita Lynn, our firstborn, Granny left the comfort of her home in Philadelphia and came to Pittsburgh to stay with us for two weeks.

She was so helpful, and Granny was old school all the way. After giving birth, the mother could not wash her hair or take a bath right away. Granny washed every inch of my body and sprayed my stitches twice a day. My hair was washed in olive oil and was pressed with a straightening comb and curled. Granny made sure that I looked like I had just stepped out of the beauty shop. Oh yes, and the cooking. I can't forget that Granny did all the cooking for those two weeks. Mmm-mmm, good—what an aroma filled the house! We were spoiled and hated to see her go back to Philadelphia.

When Granny would visit, she always let me snuggle up next to her and talk with her like I had done as a child, even though I was grown, married, and had children of my own. Granny didn't care; I was still one of her babies. She still let me stay close to her. She *never* treated me or my siblings like we weren't her natural-born children.

At the birth of our second child, Granny again came to Pittsburgh to see about me. John III was born in November of 1977. My husband's mother, Mom Bessie Ruth, also came to take care of me and our son. We had great times together; there is nothing as wonderful as family love. I was surrounded by two grandmothers and a husband during this recovery time, and they were all of the old school opinion that I should be treated like a queen. I was not allowed to do anything but nurse our new son and bond with baby John.

We had a lot of time to talk about the Lord while Granny was with us. It was at our kitchen table where my husband, John, ministered to her, and she cried unto the Lord. Granny was drawn by the Spirit of the Lord to give her heart to Jesus. Granny's November trip to Pittsburgh was unlike any other that she had ever had. When she left our city, she was taking back with her the greatest gift and blessing that she would ever receive in her life. What a wonderful evening we had! That night would always be a glorious memory in my life.

Life always has its turns, and when our third child, Mia Ruth, was born in April of 1981, Mom Bessie Ruth had recently had brain surgery. I held Mia Ruth up for Mom Bessie Ruth to see, and tears filled her eyes. Mom Bessie Ruth was not able to talk during that time, but it was clear that she was excited about and recognized that she had another granddaughter. Granny had passed prior to Mia Ruth's birth, and oh, how I missed the children's grandmothers! I felt a little sorry for myself. I was going to miss out on that special old-school love and care, and Mia Ruth would not get to know the love of her grandmothers.

Granny had taken ill soon after she left Pittsburgh in 1977, so she didn't make the trip down again. We would often talk on the phone about tips on raising children, recipes for dinner, family happenings, and just day-to-day events. Having no family members in Pittsburgh, I often got homesick, but the phone calls were the best I could do to feel like I was home and close to Granny. I would return to Philadelphia to visit home whenever I could, but having small children made it difficult, if not impossible, to just pack up and travel.

Granny's health began to get worse. I used to get on Granny at times about her health in regard to smoking. She had already begun to have a "smoker's cough." Granny would tell me that she was trying to stop. One day I got a call from Delores, Granny's daughter, to come quickly because the doctors said it would not be long. I told Shorty, as we called her, "No one ever likes to hear those words on the other end of the phone." I assured Shorty that we would be there as soon as possible.

Difficult or not, I gathered the children, and off to Philadelphia we went. My husband, John, joined us there a few days later, as soon as he could. When we arrived, I went straight to the hospital. All our family members and friends were gathered there. Granny was so sick. She had just had surgery on her lungs. I tried talking to her and telling her that the children and I were there and that I loved her.

The pain medicine Granny had been given was strong, and it seemed to make her talk strangely. She was talking about getting up to fry some fish and get the laundry off the line. A number of times, Granny said, "I see babies all over the bed." We all wished that Granny would get up and fry some fish. No one could fry fish like Granny. I'm sure we all tried our hand at Granny's recipe, but only Granny had the touch. Our fried fish was good, but it sure couldn't replace Granny's. But we weren't really interested in Granny's fish right then; we just wanted Granny to get up and get back to her life as normal.

I remember my head hurting and my heart aching when the doctors told us that Granny would not make it through the night. We did not want to believe it. We all stayed pretty late at the hospital. We didn't want to miss any time with Granny. We were waiting just to hear her say anything, even if it didn't make sense. Listening to

Granny's mumblings from that hospital bed brought a smile to my face. I longed just to hear the sound of Granny's voice, even though I knew she was passing from death to life.

It was late when we all finally left the hospital. We had stayed as long as the authorities would allow us. None of us wanted to leave, but we were basically put out. The doctors said that Granny needed to rest now and that they would contact us if there was any change.

My family stayed at Shorty's house. Shorty told me that while I was asleep, I was having a conversation with Granny. She said that throughout my sleep, I called Granny's name. Granny slipped away from us to heaven that night. On Saturday, September 8, 1979, at the age of fifty-five years, Granny, Momma Liz, Elizabeth Cobbs Butler, left me, thirteen years after my mom had left me.

The days ahead led to Granny's viewing and her funeral. A beautiful home-going service was held for her. I smiled through the pain because I remembered Granny telling me after my mom's funeral that I would not be going to any more funerals, not even hers. I smiled and said in my heart, *Granny, nothing could have kept me from being here today.* Granny's biological children and grandchildren, as well as her extended family consisting of my siblings and me and our children and spouses, were all in attendance, along with many, many friends. There were so many of us. Granny was well loved, respected, and would be missed by many.

Granny had now joined my mom, and I knew they were chattering and catching up on all the family. There I was—I had lost two moms. One might have referred to me as a motherless child, but I have learned that God can be a mother to the motherless, and He has been just that to me. I miss both of my moms dearly, even after all these years, but I have memories that sustain me. At times, when I am missing them and cry in secret, my memories of my moms are priceless.

Rosella Hurst Brown Poindexter and Elizabeth Cobbs Butler were two friends together in life, and now in death they were reunited. Two moms displayed such love that they brought two families together into one. Someone once said, "What's love got to do with it?" I say, "Everything!" Love formed and bonded our families.

God has such a wonderful plan for our lives. Jeremiah 29:11 states, "For I know the thoughts and plans that I have for you, says the Lord" (AMP).

THE FORGIVENESS PIECE

The forgiveness piece is not an easy task. If you ever have been mistreated, abused, wronged, or misunderstood, you truthfully know that it hurts and hurts deeply. No one can describe the pain you feel in words, because the pain is sometimes so very deep.

I have often heard about forgiveness in church sermons and at spiritual seminars. It has been said that if you hold on to what a person has done to you, you give the other person power over you and your life. Unforgiveness can also create bondages in your life that eat up your life. Just by holding on to unforgiveness, you can be put in a position where Satan can torment you over the thing that you won't forgive.

Katherine Claudette Campbell, provides a comprehensive perspective to consider from her teachings on forgiveness:

> You may actually feel like you have a right to not forgive your perpetrators, after all, they hurt you. You may have been innocent in that process, but you were injured, abused, damaged or hurt in any number of different ways. You are the victim, why should you be the one to forgive?

Unfortunately, many of us, "make friends," with our pains associated with trauma; especially if the trauma and pain occurred some time ago. We have become comfortable with the pain. We expect it to always be there and yes, every morning it is there to remind us of its presence. For some the pain and associated unforgiveness have been there so long that we cannot remember life prior to the offense.

Often multiple triggers feed the pain and reality of unforgiveness. Music, a word, a fragrance, a location, a season, an associated person, the person or agency or institution itself can trigger the emotion and cause the wound to bleed all over again. If you are comfortable with your pain and unforgiveness you will want to keep it and continue to massage and nurture it. But if you have reached your fill of the pain that this unforgiveness and pain has caused you, there is hope. Look at the forgiveness piece.

The first thing that you must understand from a natural and physical perspective is that FORGIVENESS IS NOT AN EMOTION! FORGIVENESS IS A COMMAND! When you DECIDE to forgive, you will be making the CHOICE TO FORGIVE!

The second thing that you must understand from a natural and physical perspective is that FORGIVENESS IS NOT TO FREE THE PERPETRATOR!

FORGIVENESS IS TO FREE YOU! Yes, you, the victim!

The first thing that you must understand from a spiritual perspective is that YOU TIE GOD'S HANDS ON YOUR BEHALF WHEN YOU WON'T FORGIVE! You tie God's hands in that He cannot forgive you. Yes, you, the victim!

The second thing that you must understand from a spiritual perspective is that the moment you CHOOSE to forgive your perpetrator, you FREE YOURSELF and you FREE GOD to work on your behalf.

Once you CHOOSE to forgive, you will be presented with a myriad of reasons why you as the victim should not have to forgive. One of the biggest reasons that will surface is the thought that your perpetrator will "get away "with their offense.

The third thing that you must understand from a spiritual perspective is that EVERY SINGLE REASON THAT SURFACES TO SUPPORT WHY YOU SHOULD NOT HAVE TO FORGIVE IS A LIE!

The enemy of your soul will try to sell you on how much you are the victim and how it was you that has been mistreated, abused, etc. You will have seemingly overwhelming proof of why you were the one hurt; you should not have to do the forgiving.

The fourth thing that you must understand from a spiritual perspective is that YOU WILL NEVER BE FREE UNTIL YOU FORGIVE!

I was holding all my pain inside. Pain does not always manifest when you are around people. You smile and interact with whatever is going on around you; you appear to be having surface fun. But when you are alone and no one sees you crying and yelling out, that's when your pain and misery surface.

Your heart aches, your mind sizzles, and your voice screams out, "Why, oh God, why?" Or your mind tries to comprehend and says, *Who would do this to innocent children?* You try to find solace in the fact of "I didn't deserve this." You seek answers to questions that you can't ask anyone. You are stuck, not knowing that you can get help, counseling, and healing through the forgiveness piece.

God saw me, and He knew my inner pain and suffering. Whenever I heard the term *foster child*, I would always seem to cringe and shrivel up inside. I could not bring myself to say the words *foster child* without tears welling up in my eyes. Sometimes, remembering the horror, turmoil, abuse, and insane treatment that I had suffered as a foster child made me want to regurgitate. For many years after Granny had rescued us from the system, I still suffered from the incredible mental and physical scars I had received as a foster child.

God showing me how much He loved me ordered my steps. One day after I had been living in Pittsburgh for quite some time, I saw a flyer pinned to a bulletin board, and this was the wording:

Were you ABUSED as a child?
Are you now an ADULT and can't
SHAKE off
What happened to you?
Turn your life around and see a counselor
FREE
To help you work through what you need!

The flyer indicated the location of the counseling and a phone number to call for more information. I thought I was seeing things. This flyer was speaking to me, though I had never known anything like this existed. I jotted down the number and called. I scheduled to meet with a therapist to discuss whatever I needed or wanted to discuss.

When I presented for the appointment, I thought it might be difficult to discuss all my abuse and horror with a stranger, but I was brimming with pain and needed it to be gone forever. With God once again showing me how much He loved me, I bonded quickly with the therapist and began to reveal what my life had been like. I started out by saying, "I was in the foster care system in Philadelphia, Pennsylvania, and it was a living nightmare!"

Every week, the therapist had me doing different types of releases. Here are a few of the things that I did: I was instructed to write letters to the people who had hurt me, to read the letters out loud and then rip them up into little pieces, and finally, to *throw the pieces away*. Also, I was instructed to draw a picture of the perpetrator. The therapist tacked the picture to the wall, and then I had to talk to the picture of the person and tell that person how I felt. That was a very heavy and emotional process. It was slow and painful, but it worked for me.

I had many layers of hurt and unforgiveness. There were a lot of healing tears and forgiveness necessary in the sessions I attended. Those sessions were so beneficial to me, and I am so glad that it was available. Session after session, I began to feel so much weight lifting off my heart and mind. Just writing the letter alone, or just reading it aloud, or just ripping up the letter and throwing it away did not totally free me. It was definitely part of the journey. Just the drawing of the perpetrator and talking to the drawing were not enough. It wasn't until the forgiveness piece entered in that I actually became free. Also, part of the process involved sessions with my husband, and he helped me walk through these therapeutic healings and extend for-giveness. It took all these components to produce a healed, delivered, and set-free Paulette Davidson.

Mrs. Carrie L. Porter, prayer coach, in her book titled *May I Pray With You?* states, Let us never confuse hurts with unforgiveness. One writer said, "hurting people — hurt people!" Hurts can be healed; however, forgiveness requires confession and repentance.

When you don't forgive a person, they have power over you. That person goes on with their life, and you are the one who remains *stuck*. You become stymied and paralyzed. You are the one who will never be able to move forward because of your past. You may be carrying around baggage of hurts and unforgiveness of something someone did to you. That baggage has turned into bondage and then to the death of your spirit man. Find your release, your freedom through God's forgiveness. Once you have received God's forgiveness and forgiven those who have hurt you, you will be able to move forward to becoming the best person God has designed you to be.

Forgiveness is worth the effort. It will change your life forever! It is due to the forgiveness piece that I was able to face the bus driver in

Philadelphia, Mr. Harrison, and not physically assault him or scream out to the passengers on his bus of the egregious ills he had made me suffer as a child. Take the time to look into the forgiveness piece. Your life will never be the same. Listen to the song sung by Israel Houghton, "Moving Forward." You will be able to move forward in your life. Expect a release! Free yourself by forgiving others!

I am so glad that help is now widely available to children and adults regarding sexual and other types of abuse. I thank God that there are public service announcements that encourage children to speak out about uncomfortable and inappropriate touching of any kind and by anyone. Making children aware of their right to be safe and protected and cared for makes it easier for children who have been abused to come forward. Education on this topic being made available in schools through talks with "safe adults," books, pamphlets, and other sources of information is a wonderful way for children and adults to receive help if someone is currently hurting them or has hurt them in the past.

Jesus has forgiven our sins. Who are we not to forgive others?

If while you are reading this, you experience the slightest tinge of an uncomfortable memory relating to past or current abuse, or you sense the need to forgive, reach out to someone for help. It is no longer necessary for you to suffer in silence. Counseling, wholeness, and forgiveness await you.

References to Forgiveness

Mathew 6:12, 14–15 reads, "Forgive us our debts as we forgive our debtors. For if we forgive men their trespasses, your heavenly

Father will also forgive you: But if ye forgive *not* men their trespasses, neither will your Father forgive *your* trespasses" (emphasis added).

Mark 11:25–26 reads, "And when you stand praying, if you hold anything against anyone, forgive them, so that your Father in heaven may forgive you your sins."

Colossians 1:14 reads, "In whom we have redemption through His blood, even the forgiveness of sins."

In the book of Luke 23:43, one thief, while on the cross, gave a last confession request, and Jesus honored his request.

Matthew 18:21–22 NASB reads, "Then Peter came and said to Him, 'Lord, how often shall my brother sin against me and I forgive him? Up to seven times?' Jesus said to him, 'I do not say to you, up to seven times, but up to seventy times seven.'"

SHENANDOAH, VIRGINIA

I'm not sure why the driving force behind finding out about Mom's roots was so incredibly strong, but it had begun to consume my nights and days. I could see that I was not about to get any peace until I satisfied that need to know about my family. I feel in my heart that Mom knew if anybody in our family ever traced our roots, it would be me. My siblings would always say to me, "What are you doing now?" They knew I was always doing something new. They thought I was being creative at something all the time.

After Mom passed, I always had a drive from within of *Who am I? What are my roots? Where did the name* Poindexter *come from?* I had enrolled in college as Paulette Poindexter, but I didn't know anyone else named Poindexter. I had so many unanswered questions, and I was determined to get some answers. I needed answers not just for me, but I also felt a responsibility to my family and siblings and to their children and to all of the Pauline Virginia Hurst Brown generations to come. One of my nieces was doing a paper in high school on family roots. Her dad told her to call me because I had found out the family history.

Here is how my search began: I contacted the Vital Statistics Office in Page County, Virginia. I provided the clerk with the names

Rosella Hurst Brown as my mother's name and *Pauline Virginia Hurst Brown* as the name of my grandmother. I acquired Mom's birth and death certificates and Grandma Pauline's death certificate. My grandmother's death certificate listed her parents as Amos Hurst and Emma Evans, both from Page County, Shenandoah, Virginia. I was ecstatic! I had just learned the names of my great-grandparents.

I was aware that census records were kept, so I went to the Carnegie Library and sent for the microfilm records for all the years that would represent where Mom's family would have been. My search took me all the way back to the 1800s. I was amazed, and it was an awesome feeling to see the names of the heads of households and their children's names. These were my relatives, blood family who had lived during that time. What a keepsake!

I was getting so excited about what I had found, and I wanted to move on. I kept finding relatives on the microfilm. Here are the names and records that I found on the census records:

Maternal side:

Lee Evans — head of household

In 1860, Lee Evans was forty years old. He was my great-grandmother's (Emma, aged thirteen) father. His wife was named Nellie Evans, and she was thirty-six. Their other children were Mary, fifteen; Florence, fourteen; Louis, twelve; Elizabeth, eight; Charles, five; and Joseph, two.

രുരുരുരു

Paternal side:

Jennie Hurst — head of household

In 1845, Jennie Hurst was fifty-four years old. She was my great-grandfather's (Amos, aged fourteen) mother. Her other children and those who lived in the household at the time were Sheridan Hurst, twelve; and David Hurst, thirty; with his wife Mary Hurst, twenty-four; and their son George Hurst, three.

ରୋରୋ

The records indicated that Amos Hurst met Emma Evans, and Pauline Virginia Hurst was born (my grandmother). Pauline met John Poindexter, and Rosella Hurst was born (my mom).

ରୋରୋ

I had the thought that maybe just maybe there was someone still living in Shenandoah who might have known my mother or grandmother. I called the authorities in Shenandoah to get the name of the local newspaper. I contacted the *Page News and Courier* of Luray, Virginia, and asked if I could put an article in the "Dear Editor" section of their newspaper.

The woman that I spoke with was warm and inviting. As she welcomed me to send the article, she assured me that they would send me an edition of the newspaper with my printed article. Just before we hung up, she wished me luck on my search.

Here is the article that was placed in the *Page News and Courier*:

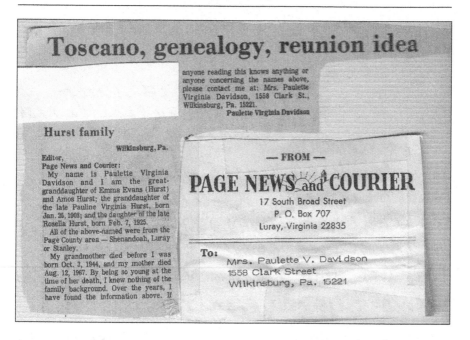

Toscano, genealogy, reunion idea

Hurst family

Wilkinsburg, Pa.

Editor,
Page News and Courier:

My name is Paulette Virginia Davidson and I am the great-granddaughter of Emma Evans (Hurst) and Amos Hurst; the granddaughter of the late Pauline Virginia Hurst, born Jan. 26, 1908; and the daughter of the late Rosella Hurst, born Feb. 7, 1925.

All of the above-named were from the Page County area — Shenandoah, Luray or Stanley.

My grandmother died before I was born Oct. 3, 1944, and my mother died Aug. 12, 1967. By being so young at the time of her death, I knew nothing of the family background. Over the years, I have found the information above. If anyone reading this knows anything or anyone concerning the names above, please contact me at: Mrs. Paulette Virginia Davidson, 1558 Clark St., Wilkinsburg, Pa. 15221.

Paulette Virginia Davidson

— FROM —

PAGE NEWS and COURIER

17 South Broad Street
P. O. Box 707
Luray, Virginia 22835

To:
Mrs. Paulette V. Davidson
1558 Clark Street
Wilkinsburg, Pa. 15221

I was delighted. I received responses from the article very quickly. One letter came from a Mrs. Ruth Staples, aged seventy-four, on October 11, 1982. Mrs. Staples related that she had grown up with my grandmother, Pauline. In fact, they had gone to school together. She then in turn had known my mother, Rosella, when she was a little girl.

Here is Mrs. Staples's letter:

504 5th Street
Shenandoah, Va. 22849
Oct. 11, 1982

Dear Paulette,

In last Thursday's paper I read your letter to the Editor of the Page News and Courier in regard to the Hurst family.

I am very happy to tell you that I knew your great-grandmother Emma, your grandmother Pauline, (I was born in 1908 alas) and I knew Rosella when she was a little girl. I did not know Amos. Pauline lived with her uncle, George David Hurst, better known as Dave. He was a brother to Amos. Dave had a son named George Hurst. George lived to be 81 years old. He died Sept. 14, 1977. He worked for my family most all his life, as long as he was able. George was well known and liked by all people in Shenandoah. He had many friends. George really loved flowers. He used to work for a Mr. Lester who raised a lot of flowers and George would bring the most beautiful roses and glads to my mother and me. Knowing his love for flowers when he passed away I sent flowers and attended his funeral also.

George was born in 1896 in Madison County. If you are interested in any other Hurst relatives perhaps if you would contact the Madison County clerk's office at the Court House, Madison, Virginia 22727, you probably could find more records of the Hurst family.

I just talked on the phone to Mrs. Hattie Mitchell. When she was young she lived with Dave Hurst's family and grew up with Pauline. She told me to tell you to come to see her. She can give you a lot of information concerning the family history. She said she would love to see you. Her address is:

Mrs. Hattie Mitchell, 714 8th Street, Shenandoah, Va. 22849

Phone No: area code 703 - 652-3348

Hattie lives just three blocks from me. I know she would be glad to hear from you. Come to see her!

If you do come to Shenandoah I would be glad for you to come by to see me. My mother was always a good friend to all your relatives. They would all come by to see us. I still live at the homeplace

Well, Paulette I feel like I almost

know you but I guess it is time to bring this to a close. I hope this letter will be some help to you. I am just glad I could write to you. Hope we can meet sometime.

Sincerely,

Ruth (Rothgeb) Staples

I also received a telephone call from Mrs. Hattie Mitchell. I believe Mrs. Mitchell was in her late seventies in October 1982. Mrs. Mitchell stated on the telephone that she had grown up in the house with my grandmother, Pauline, and remembered when my mother, Rosella, was born. This really got my juices and curiosity flowing. I felt like I had struck oil. I said to my husband, "I just have to get there and visit with these ladies."

I called both of the ladies and asked if I could come down to Virginia and talk with them to get more information on my mom's family. They both were very excited to be able to talk to Rosella's daughter. Both ladies had lost touch with my mom and grandmother after they left Virginia and moved to Harrisburg. Mrs. Mitchell did mention that she had attended Pauline's funeral, and that was the last time she had seen Rosella.

The ladies welcomed me to come down to Virginia because they wanted to meet me as much as I wanted to meet them. I asked my sisters and brothers to go with me, or my husband, but no one was free to go. It was a year and six months before I could actually get down to Virginia to meet the ladies, but we kept in touch. I didn't want them to forget about me, and I was certainly praying that they both would continue to be in good health so that I could meet them when I was able to get to Virginia.

Finally, the time was here! In June of 1984, I bravely boarded a Greyhound bus for Shenandoah, Virginia. I planned to stay for a week. I set out alone, leaving my husband and three children in Pittsburgh, to meet and go into the homes of two ladies that I did not know. My mind raced with uncertainties: *Am I crazy, going to a strange place I have never been before and by myself? Did these people really know my mom and grandmother? What are they going to tell me? Will the information be good? Will it be bad? Will I ask the right questions to get the information I need? I don't want to miss anything. Will I be safe with these people? Will I be abused again?* The questions just swirled in my head.

I decided that my need to know outweighed any of the concerns or issues or second thoughts that I might be having. I knew that God would keep me safe, so I sat back and tried to relax and enjoy the scenery on the southern bus route. Intermittently my mind wandered to the bus ride I had taken with my mom many years ago to meet Carol and Mr. Brown. The memories of that family history brought a reflective smile. Here I was on another adventure, seeking more family history. I reviewed the information discussed with Mrs. Mitchell. She had invited me to lodge at her house, and she had said that she would pick me up at the Greyhound bus station.

We were there! The driver parked the bus in the stall at the station and announced Page County, Virginia—Shenandoah, Virginia. I believe my heart skipped a beat. I was excited and apprehensive at the same time. But I had come this far, and it was too late to turn around—although I knew I would not turn around even if someone tried to drag me away. I was closer to the factual truth about my family history, and I was determined to find out whatever they were willing to disclose.

As the bus door opened, I saw an older black woman standing at the curb. When I stepped down onto the last step, the woman said, "Paulette?" I answered, "Yes." The bus was pulling away from the stall, and the woman said, "I am Mrs. Hattie Mitchell, and you sure do look like your mother, Rosella." She was smiling and beaming all in her eyes. Her smile melted all my concerns, and I knew this was going to be a treasured visit.

Mrs. Mitchell's grandson had driven her to the station and of course returned us to her home. She had already cooked dinner, so we ate as soon as we arrived at her home. The ride from the station to Mrs. Mitchell's home was pleasant, quiet, and brief. Shenandoah is a very small town. At dinner, we just talked about my bus ride, my children, and how good the food tasted.

Mrs. Mitchell showed me the room I would be staying in for the week and pointed out all the necessities. We both retired to bed, knowing the next few days would bring multiple levels of excitement all their own. As soon as I settled in, I called home to let my husband know I had arrived safely and to talk to the children.

I could hardly sleep, waiting for the next day to dawn. *Wow,* my heart pondered, *I am in the place where my mom was born and other relatives lived.* The minutes ticked away into hours and into the next morning. Obviously, at some point, I fell asleep and slept well, because I missed dawn. I was refreshed when I woke up midmorning to the wonderful aroma of Southern hospitality.

Ms. Hattie, as she told me to call her, was a great hostess. Breakfast was ready and waiting for me. Somehow it was still hot when Ms. Hattie served me. We chatted about the events for the day, such as where we would be going, who we were going to meet, some of the sights that I would see along the way—things of that nature.

Just as Ms. Hattie and I were discussing going over to Mrs. Staples's home to meet her, there was a knock on the wooden screen door. Mrs. Staples, an older white lady, could not wait to meet me. She was as excited as I was. Mrs. Staples had showed up at Ms. Hattie's house that morning in her yellow car to take us around town and to her house. We all sat there and laughed about it. We piled into Mrs. Staples's car, and she drove us to her home.

Ms. Ruth, as she welcomed me to call her, had a very big house with fourteen rooms. She said to me, "If you had started your search five years earlier, you could have met Mr. George Hurst." Mr. George was my great-grandfather's nephew. He had died in 1977 at eighty-one years of age. Ms. Ruth said that Mr. George had been the landscaper for the whole town, and he took great pride in his work. She showed me pictures of her lawn and yard, which had been the handiwork of Mr. George. She said, "Mr. George loved flowers, and the entire town loved him. So for his funeral, everyone in the town sent flowers." She knew Mr. George would have been happy, because flowers were his favorite thing.

Ms. Ruth made lunch for Ms. Hattie and me, and then she began to share her memories regarding my family. Ms. Ruth related that she and Pauline would walk together to and from school. Even though that was back in the early 1900s, it was not an unusual sight to see black and white children together in Virginia. Ms. Ruth made comments about how friendly she and my grandmother, Pauline, were.

After lunch, we got back into Ms. Ruth's fancy yellow car, and she took us on a sightseeing tour around the town of Shenandoah. Of course, Ms. Hattie, living there, was familiar with everything in the town, but they both enjoyed pointing out places that they had had interactions with my mother and grandmother.

They pointed out the post office, various business offices, the mayor's office, the grocery stores, and some other shops. They showed me the schools that they had attended or the places where those buildings had once stood. Although very small and flat, Shenandoah seemed like a nice town. The flat terrain stood out right away in contrast to the many, many hills and mountains of Pittsburgh.

Around the third or fourth day of my visit, Ms. Hattie and I were sitting on her porch, sipping iced tea and eating sandwiches. We were enjoying the nice weather during this visit. The mornings were nice and cool, and the afternoons were very warm. Although hot, the evenings offered a wonderfully warm summer breeze. Some of Ms. Hattie's grandchildren came over to meet me. She had told them about the daughter of an old friend of hers. They too wanted to meet Miss Pauline's granddaughter.

After Ms. Hattie's grandchildren left, we remained on the porch, enjoying the breeze and talking. I had brought a tape recorder with me to record any conversations about my family. I didn't want to miss any information Ms. Hattie or Ms. Ruth could tell me about my mother or grandmother.

Ms. Hattie just began to share her memories. It was wonderful to hear my life unfolding through her words. I just sat quietly listening to all that Ms. Hattie had to say. When she would pause, I would dare to jump in with a question concerning something she had just spoken about. We sat there talking like that for hours. The following memories are a part of the many, many things Mrs. Hattie Mitchell told me concerning my family.

Ms. Hattie leaned her head back on her rocking chair, closed her eyes, and just began sharing. She said, "Paulette, John Poindexter was a gentleman from Roanoke, Virginia. John worked on the Norfolk and Western Railroad. That particular line of the railroad traveled between Pennsylvania and Virginia. The men who worked the railroad would meet women at the bars and at different parties and would have a fun time. Sometimes the men would work that particular rail line one or more times a week. Other times, the men would work that particular rail line only once a month or maybe two or three times in a year. Other times, a worker might not ever repeat a particular rail line. It all depended on how the men were scheduled. The rail workers rarely had the opportunity to pick their routes until they moved up the ranks on their job.

"John Poindexter met your grandmother, Pauline, on one such occasion. After John had gone back to his job on the railroad, he returned to Pennsylvania. Pauline soon found that she was with child. Her child was Rosella, your mother. Pauline never got to see John Poindexter again, and he never got to know that he was a father. He would be up in age now, but he could be still living — nobody knows.

"As you have already learned, Pauline's parents were Amos Hurst and Emma Evans. They were never married. Pauline's mother, Emma, was living with a woman called "Old Lady Emily Ward." Old Lady Emily had a mean streak. Emma was with child, and when she went into labor, Old Lady Emily put her out of the house. Now Emma had been staying there all those months before time for her labor, pregnant and all, but Old Lady Emily put her out just when she was about to give birth to Pauline.

"No one could understand it. What on earth was Old Lady Emily thinking? Neighbors heard Emma out on Old Lady Emily's porch, crying out in pain. Someone called the midwife to come to Emma's rescue, and they tried to get her off the porch. The neighbors were trying to help Emma get to George Hurst's house, since he was Amos's nephew, but it was too late.

"Pauline was born right outside on Old Lady Emily's porch. What a horrible way to come into the world. Emma did move into George Hurst's home, though. Mr. George and his wife, Evaline, welcomed Emma and her new baby. After all, they were family. Mr. George was married three times, so I don't rightly remember which number wife

Evaline was. Evaline was a good woman, and she was my aunt. She was kind to Emma and Pauline. Amos, Pauline's father, was killed by a train here in town while Pauline was growing up. I don't remember Pauline's age around that time. A few years later, Emma married a Mr. Jim Jones, and they had lots more children.

"A lot of people lived in Mr. George's house back then. Even though it was a big house, three and four children were sleeping in one bed. You would find some of the children sprawled out at the top of the bed and some down at the bottom of the bed. Pauline was one of the many children who grew up in that house. Even when Pauline became pregnant with your mother, Rosella, they both lived in Mr. George's house. I too lived at Mr. George's house; that is how I knew your mother and grandmother.

"Mr. George drank a lot, and he would get sick at times. The men of the town would make moonshine out of the dandelion plant and other things, so they had a steady supply of liquor. Because they were always drinking, some of them lost their jobs. Because Mr. George got sick often, he only worked off and on. Aunt Evaline did not work outside of their home, and there were a lot of people in the house. There were a whole lot of mouths to feed. I stopped going to school around the age of twelve to get a job. I cleaned houses, washed dishes, and mopped floors for a dollar a week. You may think that was nothing, but I'll have you know, that was good money back then.

"Amos, Pauline's father, had a sister named Sarah. Sarah married a man with the last name Arlington, and they had three girls: Hattie, Mary, and Leona. Sarah named her daughter Hattie after me. She was a delightful child, and I loved her like she was my own. Sarah's daughter Hattie grew up and married a man with the last name of

Curry. Hattie and Mr. Curry moved to Pittsburgh. Before they left, Hattie sold me their house—yes, this very house we are now in.

"Pauline always talked about leaving Shenandoah. She wanted to get out of this small town with all of its drama. Pauline's Uncle Sheridan, her dad's brother, would visit Shenandoah frequently, and he would tell them about his life in the big city of Harrisburg. His stories sounded like an opportunity too good for Pauline to pass up. Pauline had a job, but she wanted something better for herself and her daughter, Rosella. Uncle Sheridan told Pauline there were jobs in Harrisburg and that she and her baby could stay with him and his wife.

"Your grandmother saved her money until she got enough to go to Harrisburg, and finally she and her daughter, Rosella, boarded a Greyhound bus and took off. Rosella was one and a half years old when they left Shenandoah, Virginia. Pauline met Mr. William Brown in Harrisburg, and they were married. Mr. Brown accepted Pauline's daughter, Rosella Hurst, as his own. When Rosella became old enough to start school, Mr. Brown let her use his last name. She was enrolled in school as Rosella Brown.

"Rosella came back to visit us when she was a young teenager. She loved the country. She would stay here in this house with me when she visited. Rosella did not want to go back to Harrisburg. She wanted to remain in Shenandoah with me, but Pauline would not allow it. Pauline came down to get Rosella and took her back to Harrisburg. I never saw Pauline alive again after she came to get Rosella. I attended her funeral, though, in October 1944. That was the last time I ever saw Rosella."

We talked for hours that night. Ms. Hattie had given me the history of my family as best as she could remember it. That night I mulled over Ms. Hattie's account of my family and grinned down to my toes to think that I could possibly be sleeping in the same bed that my mom had slept in as a teenager when she visited Shenandoah. How strangely things happened. Grandma Pauline wanted to leave Shenandoah and move to Harrisburg, but my mom, Rosella, wanted to leave Harrisburg and move to Shenandoah. I don't know all of what my mother's attraction was to Shenandoah, but I know part of it had to be the wonderful Southern hospitality.

The day before I was to leave, Ms. Hattie called her son and grandchildren to take me to the mall. We enjoyed a nice afternoon of shopping and spending time together. This was just another touch of Ms. Hattie's gracious hospitality. I purchased a picture frame that said "Virginia" so that I could frame some of my many memories of my time spent in my mother's birth town. I had been taking pictures all week of the various people and places.

It was time to return home. I would be boarding a Greyhound bus in the morning, and that night as I lay in the bed, I began to reflect on my visit here in Shenandoah. I had so much information about my family and great starting places to continue the search into my history. I was so excited. It didn't feel like I slept at all, although I was not tired when it was time to get up.

I awoke and got myself together and packed for the long bus ride home. We said our good-byes and promised to keep in touch with each other. Ms. Ruth drove over to Ms. Hattie's in her big yellow car to say good-bye. We three hugged warmly. They were delighted to have shared their stories, and I was delighted to have gained their knowledge. We each shed a few tears just reminiscing over the week's encounters.

The time passed quickly on the bus ride back to Pittsburgh. I kept reading and rereading the notes I had taken and listened to the stories on my tape recorder. It was so exciting to hear the ladies talk about the lives of my different relatives, even though they had passed on. Just knowing that Ms. Hattie and Ms. Ruth had been in communication with those family members was great.

I am so glad I went to visit Shenandoah and met the people who held my history in reserve until I was able to go and retrieve it. I would love to go back to visit Shenandoah and take my children and grandchildren. I would love for them to be able to see our family's home place.

My time spent in Shenandoah was a great fact-finding mission; however, it was also one great week in my life. I will always remember those days, and I hope to continue to share that experience with my other family members. I was so excited when I got back home. I showed pictures to anybody who would keep still. I shared all the information with my husband. He got the whole story from start to finish. I also told my wonderful story to my two older children and to my siblings.

My visit to Shenandoah was successful. Mommy would have been pleased with me, I am sure. We were part of a much bigger family. Although Carol had passed, DeWitt, Joyce, Marcia, Michael, and I could hold our heads high. We had family. We were not just a family of kids from nowhere. We had roots, and now we knew who our ancestors were.

As time moved onward, Ms. Hattie, Ms. Ruth, and I lost touch. The last letter and phone calls I received from them were around Christmas of 1984. I am not sure if they are still living. They were very much in their senior years back in 1982 when I first met with them. If they are still alive, they would be over one hundred years old as of this writing.

During my visit to Shenandoah, I mentioned that I wanted to write a book about my life and legacy. Both ladies greatly encouraged me to do so. Ms. Hattie said, "Yes, by all means, you should write a book about your family." Ms. Ruth said, "Yes do it." I dedicate this chapter to both of them, Mrs. Hattie Mitchell and Mrs. Ruth Staples.

Years later, after a visit with my brother Michael in Camp Hill Prison, my family also stopped by to visit Mr. Brown, who still lived in Oberlin. Camp Hill and Oberlin are nearby cities in Pennsylvania. Of course, Michael has been released from Camp Hill for several years as of this writing.

Mr. Brown greeted us with a broad smile and introduced us to his third wife. I introduced my husband and our four children to my step-grandfather, and we all had a great visit. We talked quite a bit about Grandma Pauline, their life together, and about her being sick and in the hospital for a long time.

I asked Mr. Brown if he had any pictures of Grandma Pauline. She had actually been his first wife. Mr. Brown stated, "I do believe I do. Just let me check in the attic." Mr. Brown returned with a single picture of Mrs. Pauline Virginia Hurst Brown taken before she had become ill. "Pauline died shortly after this picture was taken," he said. He was glad to give me a picture of my grandmother.

Years later I learned that Mr. Brown died at the full age of ninety-four. He outlived all three of his wives. Our step-granddad, Mr. Brown, had never had any biological children of his own, but many generations to come will carry his name.

After looking at the photo and experiencing a flood of thoughts and memories of the stories I had learned, I showed the picture to my husband and children. My children thought Grandma Pauline looked like me and our son, John III. I was incredibly delighted to see and be able to keep that photo, because I had never seen any picture of Grandma Pauline. It was glorious to be able to put a beautiful face with the wonderful history and stories that I had collected concerning my grandmother. This was just one more piece of the wonderful tapestry of the Pauline Virginia Hurst Brown legacy.

AFTERWORD

When I reflect on the writing of this tapestry of my past, I see the hand of God painting every stroke with Jeremiah 1:5: "Before I formed you in the womb I knew and approved you" (AMP). In the natural things of life, we know many, many things. The sun is yellow, the ocean is wide, most grass is green, and flowers bloom in spring. The list goes on and on.

But who knows the plan of God? *God Himself!* That's exciting. Wow, He knew me, and long before my mom answered the "Room for Rent" sign ninety years ago, He himself set Jeremiah 29:11 in motion for my life: "'For I know the plans I have for you,' declares the Lord" (NIV).

Woven into that plan were hurts, pain, tears, scars, loneliness, and many challenges. Oh, but the joy of salvation through Jesus Christ! He poured His love into all of what would form and shape my life. He silenced all the stereotypes and negative sayings that went along with the life I experienced as a child.

Before I began my search of my mom's family, I felt like I could be related to anyone. Whenever I looked at someone, I wondered, *Are we related?* Not knowing your roots can take your life on an emotional roller-coaster ride. If your eyes fell on a name from your family tree while you read this book, just say, *"We are family!"*

I received a *DaySpring* birthday card one year, and it spoke deeply into my life:

God made you on purpose.
You're not an
Afterthought,
You're not on earth
"Just because,"
And you're not a random
Act of His creativity.
You were given His 100%
Stamp of approval
From head to toe before
You were born.
And the moment you were,
He beamed with joy.
Just look at you now . . .
God must be
Smiling still.

To God be the glory for the great things He has done!
Be blessed!

ABOUT THE AUTHOR

F irst Lady Paulette V. Davidson is a native of Philadelphia, Pennsylvania, but now resides in Penn Hills, Pennsylvania. Reverend Davidson, known affectionately to some as "Sister P," received Christ as her Lord and Savior at the age of fourteen under the ministry of Reverend R. W. Schambach in West Philadelphia, Pennsylvania, at Miracle Temple Church. Sister P is Holy Ghost filled and believes in the power of God. Sister P received her prophetic mantle of drama during her teenage years with the Evelyn Graves Drama Association in 1968, which is now located in Yeadon, Pennsylvania.

Sister P is married to Pastor John T. Davidson, Jr. Their five beautiful children are Tonita Lynn, John Thomas III, Mia Ruth Hines, Erik Hines (their wonderful son-in-law), and Paulette Elizabeth. Pastor John and Sister P have three grandchildren: Amara Tomihn Davidson, Erik Michael Hines II, and Nathanael Zamar Davidson. They give glory and honor to God for the lives of their children and grandchildren.

Sister P was a former member and drama director/instructor of the Edwin Hawkins Music and Arts Seminar, Pittsburgh, Pennsylvania chapter from 1985 to 1993. She performed in drama productions held in Pittsburgh, McKeesport, and Philadelphia, Pennsylvania; Los Angeles, California; Washington, D.C.; and Rochester, New York. Reverend Davidson has written a variety of children's messages that can be used for children's ministry occasions. She is aspiring to publish her children's Christmas story, "The Light Through the Windows." Several of her poems are published in the *Different Drummer* poetry publication magazine of Community College of Allegheny County in Pittsburgh, Pennsylvania.

Sister P holds educational degrees in early childhood education and communications journalism. She is a graduate of the Marilyn J. Davis International School of the Bible in Pittsburgh, Pennsylvania. Reverend Davidson has had the opportunity to minister the Word of God and to usher others into times of praise and worship in McKeesport, Pittsburgh, and surrounding areas. God has used her mightily, and many lives have been changed. To God be the glory for the great things He has done!

Sister P is the founder of Heartstrings Ministries, ministering to people's minds, bodies, and souls. She finds joy working in the ministry and has found her destiny. Her passions are singing, writing, and producing Christian dramas. The titles of some of her dramas and skits are as follows: *Make a Way for Me, Lord; 'Me and You, Lord;' 'Worship and Praise;' It's Time; 'I'll Trade a Lifetime;' 'A Tribute to Mothers;' 'A Daughter's Confession;' 'The Life of Madam C. J. Walker;' The Black Church; Who Put Christ Out in the Cold?; Wake Up; Oh, Freedom; I Remember Mama; No Room for Jesus in Our Hearts; Praise Is What I Do; Momma's Kitchen;* and her latest production, *What to Do in a Dead Situation—The Modern-Day Story of Lazarus.*

Sister P shares almost forty-two years of ministry with her husband as they currently Co-pastor at Creative Ministries Berachah, Inc., located in McKeesport, Pennsylvania, where she serves in the following areas: co-pastor, leadership training, new membership classes, director of the women's ministry, and co-director of the marriage ministry.

Sister P likes to journal, bowl, travel, watch Family Feud, and The Chase, game shows, and all the TV judge shows. She also enjoys watching movies and TV featuring black actors. Sister P is a collector of hearts and scarves.

LIFE MESSAGES OF REV. PAULETTE V. DAVIDSON

What doth it profit a man to gain the whole world and lose his soul? Only what you do for Christ will last.

I give all the glory to Jesus Christ, who saved, healed, and delivered my life.

I love the Lord, not only for all the many wonderful things He has done in and for *my life*, but because *He loved me first* ! ✠✠✠

APPRECIATION

I thank and praise God for allowing me to come this far by FAITH!
I know it was God and along with all my family and friends that
When they heard my story said, "Girl you should write a book" or
"Sis P write that book" or "Follow your Dream"
That sparkle pushed me into the Destiny God had for me
and
Your encouragement and prayers got me through the process
A special thanks to my husband, children and church family for
All of their love, prayers, support, and believing in me
I LOVE YOU ALL – THANK YOU!

CPSIA information can be obtained at www.ICGtesting.com
Printed in the USA
BVOW06s1619241115

428239BV00004B/5/P

9 781498 450478